The Beginner's Guide to

Classic Motorcycle Restoration

Also from Veloce Publishing –

Enthusiast's Restoration Manual Series
Beginner's Guide to Classic Motorcycle Restoration YOUR step-by-step guide to setting up a workshop, choosing a project, dismantling, sourcing parts, renovating & rebuilding classic motorcycles from the 1970s & 1980s, The (Burns)
Citroën 2CV, How to Restore (Porter)
Classic Large Frame Vespa Scooters, How to Restore (Paxton)
Classic Car Bodywork, How to Restore (Thaddeus)
Classic British Car Electrical Systems (Astley)
Classic Car Electrics (Thaddeus)
Classic Cars, How to Paint (Thaddeus)
Ducati Bevel Twins 1971 to 1986 (Falloon)
How to restore Honda Fours – YOUR step-by-step colour illustrated guide to complete restoration (Burns)
Jaguar E-type (Crespin)
Reliant Regal, How to Restore (Payne)
Triumph TR2, 3, 3A, 4 & 4A, How to Restore (Williams)
Triumph TR5/250 & 6, How to Restore (Williams)
Triumph TR7/8, How to Restore (Williams)
Volkswagen Beetle, How to Restore (Tyler)
VW Bay Window Bus (Paxton)
Yamaha FS1-E, How to Restore (Watts)

Essential Buyer's Guide Series
Alfa Romeo Alfasud (Metcalfe)
Alfa Romeo Alfetta: all saloon/sedan models 1972 to 1984 & coupé models 1974 to 1987 (Metcalfe)
Alfa Romeo Giulia GT Coupé (Booker)
Alfa Romeo Giulia Spider (Booker)
Audi TT (Davies)
Audi TT Mk2 2006 to 2014 (Durnan)
Austin-Healey Big Healeys (Trummel)
BMW Boxer Twins (Henshaw)
BMW E30 3 Series 1981 to 1994 (Hosier)
BMW GS (Henshaw)
BMW X5 (Saunders)
BMW Z3 Roadster (Fishwick)
BMW Z4: E85 Roadster and E86 Coupé including M and Alpina 2003 to 2009 (Smitheram)
BSA 350, 441 & 500 Singles (Henshaw)
BSA 500 & 650 Twins (Henshaw)
BSA Bantam (Henshaw)
Choosing, Using & Maintaining Your Electric Bicycle (Henshaw)
Citroën 2CV (Paxton)
Citroën DS & ID (Heilig)
Cobra Replicas (Ayre)
Corvette C2 Sting Ray 1963-1967 (Falconer)
Datsun 240Z 1969 to 1973 (Newlyn)
DeLorean DMC-12 1981 to 1983 (Williams)
Ducati Bevel Twins (Falloon)
Ducati Desmodue Twins (Falloon)
Ducati Desmoquattro Twins – 851, 888, 916, 996, 998, ST4 1988 to 2004 (Falloon)
FIAT 124 Spider & Pininfarina Azzura Spider, (AS-DS) 1966 to 1985 (Robertson)
Fiat 500 & 600 (Bobbitt)
Ford Capri (Paxton)
Ford Escort Mk1 & Mk2 (Williamson)
Ford Focus Mk1 RS & ST170, 1st Generation (Williamson)
Ford Model A – All Models 1927 to 1931 (Buckley)
Ford Model T – All models 1909 to 1927 (Barker)
Ford Mustang – First Generation 1964 to 1973 (Cook)
Ford Mustang – Fifth Generation (2005-2014) (Cook)
Ford RS Cosworth Sierra & Escort (Williamson)
Harley-Davidson Big Twins (Henshaw)
Hillman Imp (Morgan)
Hinckley Triumph triples & fours 750, 900, 955, 1000, 1050, 1200 – 1991-2009 (Henshaw)
Honda CBR FireBlade (Henshaw)
Honda CBR600 Hurricane (Henshaw)
Honda SOHC Fours 1969-1984 (Henshaw)
Jaguar E-Type 3.8 & 4.2 litre (Crespin)
Jaguar E-type V12 5.3 litre (Crespin)
Jaguar Mark 1 & 2 (All models including Daimler 2.5-litre V8) 1955 to 1969 (Thorley)
Jaguar New XK 2005-2014 (Thorley)
Jaguar S-Type – 1999 to 2007 (Thorley)
Jaguar X-Type – 2001 to 2009 (Thorley)
Jaguar XJ-S (Crespin)
Jaguar XJ6, XJ8 & XJR (Thorley)
Jaguar XK 120, 140 & 150 (Thorley)
Jaguar XK8 & XKR (1996-2005) (Thorley)
Jaguar/Daimler XJ 1994-2003 (Crespin)
Jaguar/Daimler XJ40 (Crespin)
Jaguar/Daimler XJ6, XJ12 & Sovereign (Crespin)
Kawasaki Z1 & Z900 (Orritt)
Lancia Delta HF 4WD & Integrale (Baker)
Land Rover Discovery Series 1 (1989-1998) (Taylor)
Land Rover Discovery Series 2 (1998-2004) (Taylor)
Land Rover Series I, II & IIA (Thurman)
Land Rover Series III (Thurman)
Lotus Elan, S1 to Sprint and Plus 2 to Plus 2S 130/5 1962 to 1974 (Vale)
Lotus Europa, S1, S2, Twin-cam & Special 1966 to 1975 (Vale)
Lotus Seven replicas & Caterham 7: 1973-2013 (Hawkins)
Mazda MX-5 Miata (Mk1 1989-97 & Mk2 98-2001) (Crook)
Mazda RX-8 (Parish)
Mercedes-Benz 190: all 190 models (W201 series) 1982 to 1993 (Parish)
Mercedes-Benz 280-560SL & SLC (Bass)
Mercedes-Benz G-Wagen (Greene)
Mercedes-Benz Pagoda 230SL, 250SL & 280SL roadsters & coupés (Bass)
Mercedes-Benz S-Class W126 Series (Zoporowski)
Mercedes-Benz S-Class Second Generation W116 Series (Parish)
Mercedes-Benz SL R129-series 1989 to 2001 (Parish)
Mercedes-Benz SLK (Bass)
Mercedes-Benz W123 (Parish)
Mercedes-Benz W124 – All models 1984-1997 (Zoporowski)
MG Midget & A-H Sprite (Horler)
MG TD, TF & TF1500 (Jones)
MGA 1955-1962 (Crosier)
MGB & MGB GT (Williams)
MGF & MG TF (Hawkins)
Mini (Paxton)
Morgan 4/4 (Benfield)
Morgan Plus 4 (Benfield)
Morris Minor & 1000 (Newell)
Moto Guzzi 2-valve big twins (Falloon)
New Mini (Collins)
Norton Commando (Henshaw)
Peugeot 205 GTI (Blackburn)
Piaggio Scooters – all modern two-stroke & four-stroke automatic models 1991 to 2016 (Willis)
Porsche 356 (Johnson)
Porsche 911 (964) (Streather)
Porsche 911 (991) (Streather)
Porsche 911 (993) (Streather)
Porsche 911 (996) (Streather)
Porsche 911 (997) – Model years 2004 to 2009 (Streather)
Porsche 911 (997) – Second generation models 2009 to 2012 (Streather)
Porsche 911 Carrera 3.2 (Streather)
Porsche 911SC (Streather)
Porsche 924 – All models 1976 to 1988 (Hodgkins)
Porsche 928 (Hemmings)
Porsche 930 Turbo & 911 (930) Turbo (Streather)
Porsche 944 (Higgins)
Porsche 981 Boxster & Cayman (Streather)
Porsche 986 Boxster (Streather)
Porsche 987 Boxster and Cayman 1st generation (2005-2009) (Streather)
Porsche 987 Boxster and Cayman 2nd generation (2009-2012) (Streather)
Range Rover – First Generation models 1970 to 1996 (Taylor)
Range Rover – Second Generation 1994-2001 (Taylor)
Range Rover – Third Generation L322 (2002-2012) (Taylor)
Reliant Scimitar GTE (Payne)
Rolls-Royce Silver Shadow & Bentley T-Series (Bobbitt)
Rover 2000, 2200 & 3500 (Marrocco)
Royal Enfield Bullet (Henshaw)
Subaru Impreza (Hobbs)
Sunbeam Alpine (Barker)
Triumph 350 & 500 Twins (Henshaw)
Triumph Bonneville (Henshaw)
Triumph Herald & Vitesse (Ayre)
Triumph Spitfire and GT6 (Ayre)
Triumph Stag (Mort)
Triumph Thunderbird, Trophy & Tiger (Henshaw)
Triumph TR2 & TR3 - All models (including 3A & 3B) 1953 to 1962 (Conners)
Triumph TR4/4A & TR5/250 - All models 1961 to 1968 (Child & Battyll)
Triumph TR6 (Williams)
Triumph TR7 & TR8 (Williams)
Triumph Trident & BSA Rocket III (Rooke)
TVR Chimaera and Griffith (Kitchen)
TVR S-series (Kitchen)
Velocette 350 & 500 Singles 1946 to 1970 (Henshaw)
Vespa Scooters – Classic 2-stroke models 1960-2008 (Paxton)
Volkswagen Bus (Copping)
Volkswagen Transporter T4 (1990-2003) (Copping/Cservenka)
VW Golf GTI (Copping)
VW Beetle (Copping)
Volvo 700/900 Series (Beavis)
Volvo P1800/1800S, E & ES 1961 to 1973 (Murray)

www.veloce.co.uk

First published in July 2014, reprinted November 2020 by Veloce Publishing Limited, Veloce House, Parkway Farm Business Park, Middle Farm Way, Poundbury, Dorchester DT1 3AR, England. Tel 01305 260068 Fax 01305 268864 / e-mail info@veloce.co.uk / web www.veloce.co.uk or www.velocebooks.com.
ISBN: 978-1-845846-44-2. UPC: 6-36847-04644-6
© Ricky Burns and Veloce Publishing 2014 & 2020. All rights reserved. With the exception of quoting brief passages for the purpose of review, no part of this publication may be recorded, reproduced or transmitted by any means, including photocopying, without the written permission of Veloce Publishing Ltd. Throughout this book logos, model names and designations, etc, have been used for the purposes of identification, illustration and decoration. Such names are the property of the trademark holder as this is not an official publication. Readers with ideas for automotive books, or books on other transport or related hobby subjects, are invited to write to the editorial director of Veloce Publishing at the above address. British Library Cataloguing in Publication Data - A catalogue record for this book is available from the British Library. Typesetting, design and page make-up all by Veloce Publishing Ltd on Apple Mac. Printed and bound by CPI Group (UK) Ltd, Croydon, CR0 4YY.

ENTHUSIAST'S RESTORATION MANUAL™

The Beginner's Guide to
Classic Motorcycle Restoration

Ricky Burns

VELOCE PUBLISHING
THE PUBLISHER OF FINE AUTOMOTIVE BOOKS

Contents

Introduction 6

1. Work area 8
Safety 8
   Ventilation 9
   Children & animals 9
   Comfort 9

2. Tools & equipment 12
Spanners/wrenches, sockets &
   screwdrivers 12
Hammers 13
Craft knife 14
Pliers 14
Taps, dies, drills, and thread repair .. 15
   Bolt and stud extractors 15
   Thread repair kit 15
   Tap and die set 15
Power tools 16
   Miscellaneous items 17

3. Choosing your first project 19
Budget & time 19
Different types of projects 21
   The original restoration 21
   The show restoration 22
   The café racer 22
   The special 22
Check list 22
   First impressions 23
   The engine 23
   If the engine does not start 23
   The tank and seat 24

   Frame and forks 24

4. Sourcing parts 26
The internet 26
Clubs and forums 26
Magazines 27
The auto jumble 27

5. Getting started 29
Starting the stripdown 30
Removing the engine 32

6. Cleaning & polishing 40
Safety tips before you begin 40
Degreasing 40
Ultrasonic cleaning 40
Equipment 41
Metal polishing wheels and
   compounds 42
   Polishing compounds 42
   Polishing mops 42
   Chrome polishing 43
Rust removal 43
DIY chrome plating 45

7. The engine 46
Engine unit 48
What you will need 48
What to look for on an external
   inspection 48
What to look for on a semi-internal
   inspection 49
2-stroke engines 50

4-stroke engines 53
The bottom end 55

8. Brakes, wheels & tyres 57
Hydraulic disc brakes 57
   Rebuilding the brake calliper 57
   Rebuilding the master cylinder 60
Cable or rod drum brakes 62
   Oiling cables 62
Wheels 63
Tyres 64

9. Fuel system & exhaust 67
The fuel tank 67
Fuel tap 68
The carburettor 70
The exhaust system 74

10. Electrics 77
Faults and precautions 77
The battery 78
Wiring diagrams 78
Ignition systems 80
Charging and starting systems 82

11. Spraying, decals & badges 84
Tools and materials you will need . 84
   Preparation 85
   Priming 85
   Finish coat 85
Stripping paint 85
Decals 87
   The main rules 88

CONTENTS

Badges... 90

12. Clocks & switches 91
   Clocks and gauges...................... 94

13. Seat... 98

14. Forks 105

15. The rebuild............................. 110
   Frame build and rear end............ 110
   Rebuilding the front end............. 113
   Fitting the front wheel................. 120

Fitting the rear wheel................... 121
Refitting the engine. 123
Fitting the exhaust...................... 128

16. Getting ready for the road 131
   Cables.. 131
   Brake lights................................. 132
   Mirrors.. 132
   Tyre pressure and tread............... 133
   Split pins...................................... 133
   Lights 133
      Bulbs below 850mm from the ground.. 133

      Bulbs above 850mm from the ground.. 133
   First start-up 133
   The first ride................................ 134

17. Riding safely 135
   A country road story................... 135
   Overtaking 136
   Bad road conditions 136
   Training 137

Index... 143

Introduction

Ever since I was in my early teens, when a friend of mine was given an old Raleigh Runabout moped to ride in a field, I have been fascinated with motorcycles.

I remember my grandmother giving us 50 pence to go to the local garage to buy some petrol, and our first attempt at starting the little moped. The excitement I felt when it actually fired and came to life has never left me. We spent long sunny days riding it in a local field. The thought of something actually pulling me along or up a hill was quite fascinating.

After a few weeks we found a Honda SS50 – this was great, my first bike with gears. With no lessons on what to do with a clutch or gears, it took lots of trial and error to get us going, and although the little Honda was only 50cc, we felt it was a real motorbike.

On Sundays we would walk through the streets watching old men wash their cars, in the hope that we could see an old motorbike at the back of their garage or garden shed that they might want to sell to us. We found many old bikes this way, and most didn't take too much to get going. Those early days of motorcycling fuelled my interest and enthusiasm to this day.

When he was younger, my father had an interest in motocross, or scrambling as it was called then. He took me, my brother, and a few friends to scrambles whenever he could in the back of his work van. The smell of Castrol R on race days was great. My father broke his leg while scrambling, so, although we liked to watch the racing, he thought it a little too fast for us to compete in.

One day while in my local newsagent, I bought the first ever edition of *Trials and Motocross News*. Thereafter I bought every copy I could for quite some time, and subsequently attended some trials events.

Dad eventually bought a brand new 250cc Bultaco Sherpa. That was some bike. I learnt to ride it like it was a part of me, and I loved every minute of it.

I left school at 16, and bought an almost new Suzuki AP50 after borrowing £160 from my much loved nan, paying her back weekly from my wages. I passed my motorcycle test first time at the age of 17. One day, on my way home from work, I saw another, bigger Suzuki in my local garage. This time it was a GT185, with electric start. By now all my friends had Suzuki or Yamaha 250s. These were a little out of my price range, so I part exchanged my AP50 for the GT185, with money borrowed from my grandad this time. This was much more powerful, and I rode it regularly to race meetings at Brands Hatch circuit in Kent.

My era is the 1970s, with its wonderful assortment of crazy 2-strokes, and the first multi-cylinder superbikes coming thick and fast from Japan. The competition between manufactures to show their engineering advances was a time in motorcycle history unlikely ever to be repeated.

I remember longing for the new bikes on display at the motorcycle shows in Earl's Court and Olympia. Bikes that, at the time, were way over an apprentice engineer's budget, can now be found on auction websites just waiting to be restored.

My aim is not to go into depth on every aspect of restoring a motorcycle. A complete book could be written about each chapter. This book has been written to guide the first time restorer through his or her first project, from purchase to riding. Because this book is primarily a guide to restoration,

INTRODUCTION

it should be used in conjunction with the appropriate workshop manual for your motorcycle.

Whilst writing this book, I worked on my newest project – a 1976 Suzuki GT750, also known as the 'Kettle' or 'Water Buffalo.' In the first photos I saw of this motorcycle, it looked quite reasonable. However, once it arrived home, it became clear there was more to this project than I first thought. This is typical when embarking on a task such as motorcycle restoration. You come across many unexpected problems. My aim is to help you overcome these, and save you time and money by avoiding common mistakes and pitfalls.

Good luck with your project.

Left for years and scorched by the Colorado sun ...

... after 6 months' work this little Honda looks and rides like new again.

Chapter 1
Work area

Before you begin looking for your project, or begin work on one you already own, set up and organise your work area. It's more likely that you will succeed in finishing your project and achieve a good result if you are comfortable where you are working.

To begin with, establish where the workshop is going to be: is there access to a garage, shed or even a spare room? If so, is it big enough? An area outside the house is going to be more suitable, given the smells and noises that come from carrying out a restoration.

The working area needs to be organised, of a comfortable temperature, with good lighting, and above all it must be safe. Addressing areas such as draughts, insulation, lighting, heating, and shelving or racking for storage, will help make work much easier. You need to know where you put things and how to find them quickly. If your fingers are cold and the light is dim, your project is going to take longer, and you could lose interest very quickly.

If you do not already have a work bench, you will need one now! It needs to be strong enough to hold an engine. Either buy one – it will have a maximum weight shown – or make one. If making a bench, make it as sturdy and safe as you can – it needs to withstand the weight of your engine and other equipment. You may only be working on a small 100cc Yamaha this time, but if you go on to do another restoration, your could be dealing with a hefty Honda Goldwing engine! Length is also important: bolt down your pillar drill, bench grinder, and vice.

Should you choose to make your own workbench there are free plans available on the internet, and they provide a lot of detail. The main point is to make it strong and sturdy. The size will depend on the space available, but try for a minimum of 600mm (2 foot) deep and 1m (3 foot) high. Wooden fence posts are strong and economical for the legs, and get some 100mm x 50mm (4in x 2in) wood from your local DIY store and a sheet of 25mm (1 inch) plywood for the worktop. Use either coach bolts or decent sized crosshead screws to bolt everything together.

SAFETY

Accidents do happen, so ensure you do everything possible to avoid them. Also, remember that safety precautions apply not only to you, but to anyone else who is present in the workshop. Following a few simple rules every time you work on your project will make work easier

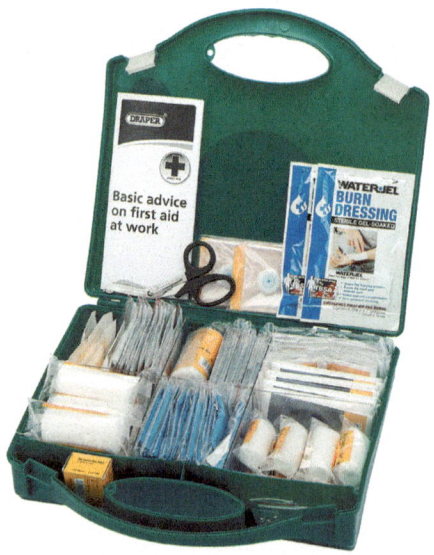

1.1 Begin by ensuring you have a first aid kit. They are very inexpensive, and are essential in a working environment. You will have hand tools, machines and chemicals to deal with, and any one of these can cause injury. Ensure you are prepared.

WORK AREA

and quicker, and once they become a habit, it will not feel like a chore.

Once you begin work, ensure you keep the workshop as clean and tidy as possible. It's easy to get carried away and end up with a cluttered work area. Put tools away at the end of the day – not only will you know where they are next time, the work area will stay trip-hazard free. Trips and falls are high on the most common accident list, and are easily avoided if the floor is kept tidy.

If you are working on your project alone, it might be worth getting someone to check on you occasionally to ensure you are okay. Some tasks involve lifting or using machinery – get someone to assist if needed.

The book highlights safety equipment necessary for each task. Safety equipment is not expensive, is widely available, and must be used. Read each chapter before you begin the task to ensure you have all the necessary safety equipment. Never avoid wearing safety equipment that can prevent serious injury. It has been designed to protect you – wearing it could ensure you never have to go to the accident and emergency department.

Next, remember to keep all combustible items away from sparks. Have a fixed place to store fuel cans, thinners and paints, well away from grinders etc.

Ventilation
Paints, paint-strippers, solvents, and other chemicals can fill the air with fumes and contaminants that are highly combustible, deadly to breathe, or both. It is essential, in whatever space you choose, that there is sufficient ventilation to remove harmful gases, fumes, and dust. It's a good idea to install a fan to vent air to the outside and replace it with fresh air.

CAUTION! Even in well-ventilated areas, it is essential to wear protective respirators or air-filters when working with a substance that generates harmful fumes or dust.

Children & animals
If you have young children and animals, restrict access to your workshop. At the very least, place all tools and hazardous chemicals in locked cabinets when not in use. Children should never have unsupervised access to workshops, tools or equipment at any time.

COMFORT
Simple things placed on the floor, like flattened cupboard boxes or an old piece of carpet, will help keep feet warm on cold winter days, and are not expensive. There are some good quality space heaters available that are well worth considering. They warm up large areas quickly, but can be a little noisy. Alternatively, if you want to keep your workshop at a constant temperature, oil-filled radiators have built in thermostats and run almost silently.

Fit some draught excluder around

1.5 Make a fire extinguisher a part of your workshop. You will be using petrol, oils, paints and thinners – all highly flammable liquids. Get a multi-purpose dry powder extinguisher. These are best for fires involving solids and liquids, such as grease, fats, oils, paint, petrol, etc.

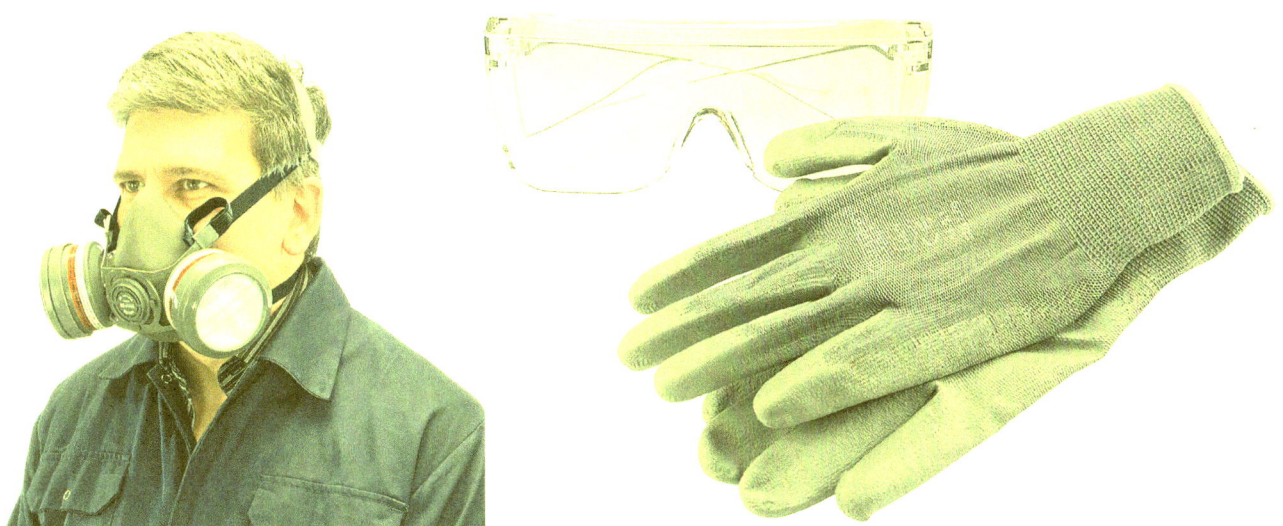

1.2, 1.3, 1.4 Remember to wear safety goggles, gloves, and a face mask when appropriate.

CLASSIC MOTORCYCLE RESTORATION

1.6 In colder climates and in winter months, a small electric space heater heats up a large area quickly.

all the doors and window frames. This keeps the workshop warmer, and saves on heating costs, too. Consider insulating the roof – this is where heat will escape, and if it is insulated you will stay warmer for longer.

If you are lucky enough to live in a warmer climate, I for one envy you. Keep good ventilation and plenty of drinks available, but leave the beer until you have finished working. A friend of mine came to help me lift out an engine one time and he could hardly hold himself up, let alone an engine.

The use of small domestic containers such as washed out plastic margarine tubs with lids or old jam jars, together with a simple labelling system, will help keep everything organised and will not add to the cost of your project. After all, you want to spend any available funds on the project itself.

It will help in the long run if you have a designated area just for the project, with as much space as possible. When it is time to strip the bike, put the parts away in an organised fashion – this will help you locate the parts easily when rebuilding. Some strong shelving for the heavier parts and a racking system for the

1.7 Small organisers are great for storing nuts and bolts and other small items, and labelling the drawers makes it quicker and easy to find what you need when you need it.

1.8 A low-cost set of shelves helps ensure a tidy workshop, and frees up floor space.

WORK AREA

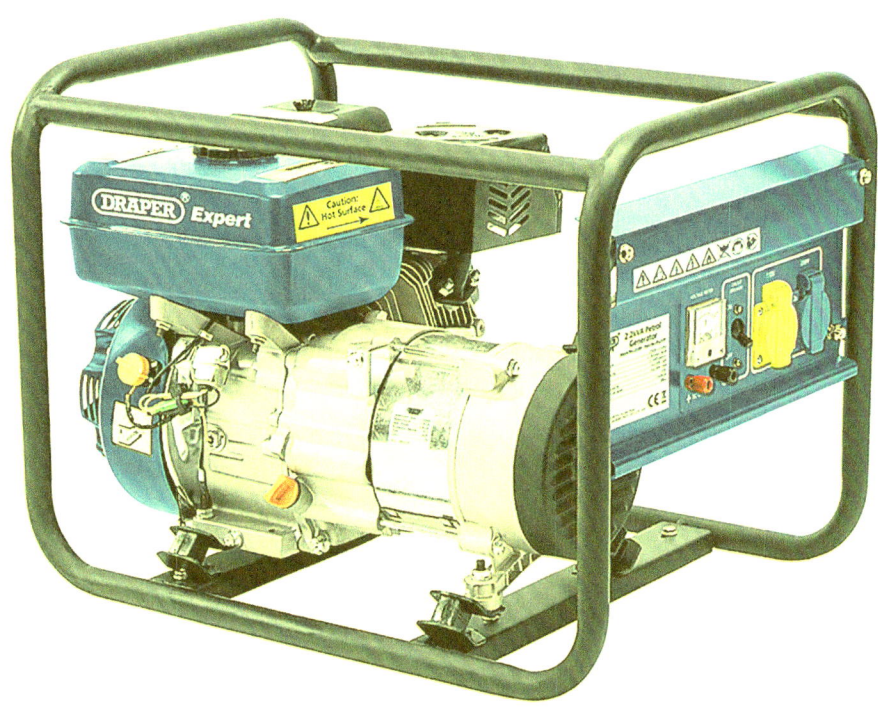

smaller parts will help keep the floor space clear for work times.

Ideally, get an electrical supply for power tools, heaters and lighting. If you have a detached garage or shed you can always use a small generator for lighting and recharging battery hand tools, but most readers will have a power source already installed.

1.9 A small generator is needed if you do not have an electrical supply, but remember it must be used outside – the exhaust fumes contain deadly carbon monoxide.

Chapter 2
Tools & equipment

Your restoration project will be much easier with the correct tools to hand.

In this section we go through the tools and equipment needed for your restoration. Assess what you already have: will it do the job, or is it just going to hinder your efforts? If you do need to buy tools, buy the best you can afford. You do not have to get brand new tools – well-made secondhand tools will be cheaper and as effective.

Check your local hire shop for tools only needed for odd jobs, such as a torque wrench, or maybe borrow from a friend.

The amount of work you are happy to carry out yourself will dictate which tools are needed. For instance, if you intend to send the fuel tank and other painted items to a professional sprayer, you will not need any spray equipment. Likewise, if you're asking an engineer to rebuild the engine, than you will not need engine specific tools.

Some engine work requires specialist tools. These tools are bike specific, and are not listed here. In many cases there are ways around using the specialist tools, but this will make some tasks harder to carry out.

This is the minimum needed:
A selection of spanners
A selection of sockets
A set of different sized screwdrivers
Allen keys
Wire cutters and pliers
Stanley knife
Club hammer
Rubber hammer
Circlip pliers
Feeler gauges
Some wire brushes
Bench vice
Torque wrench
Safety goggles and gloves, masks etc
Hacksaw

SPANNERS/WRENCHES, SOCKETS & SCREWDRIVERS

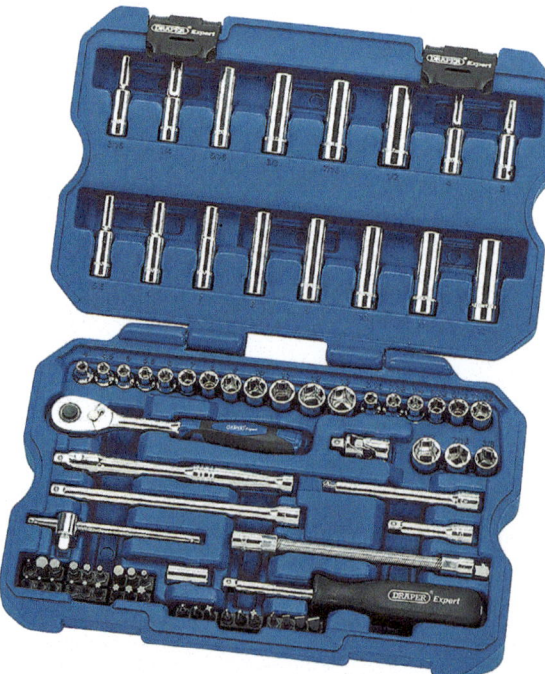

2.1 These are going to be the tools that you use for the vast majority of jobs, with some sizes used frequently. On Japanese or European bikes you will use a 10mm, 13mm and 14mm spanner/wrench or socket on almost every task. If your project is an American model or an old British bike, you will need an imperial set of spanners and sockets.

TOOLS & EQUIPMENT

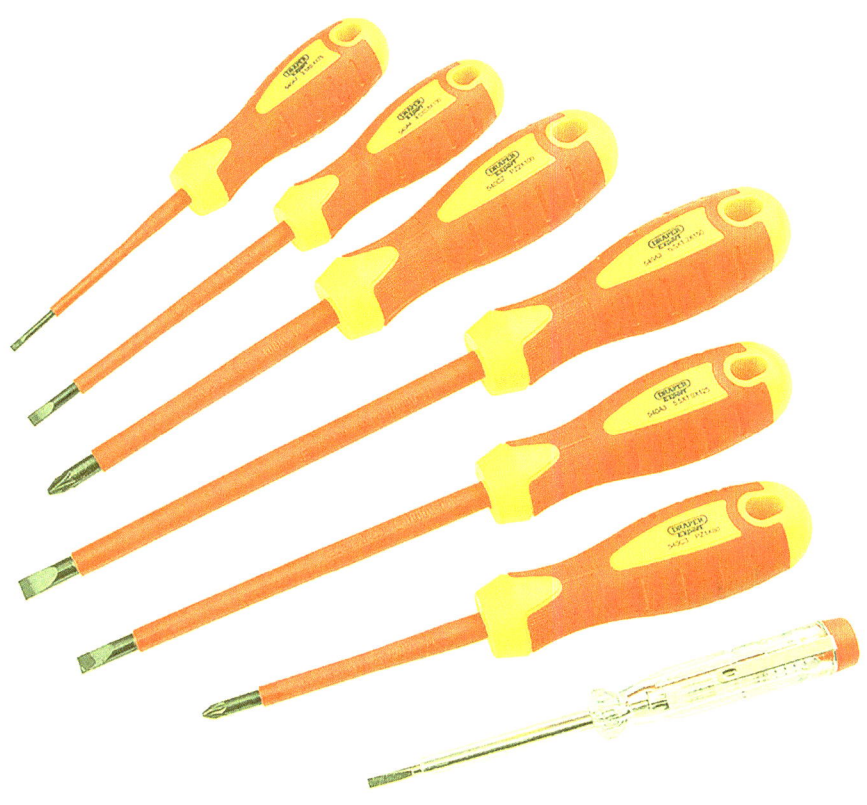

2.2 A good set of flatblade and crosshead screwdrivers is essential on any project. Buy a set with an good assortment of sizes. Magnetic blades are useful for fishing out small screws that have dropped.

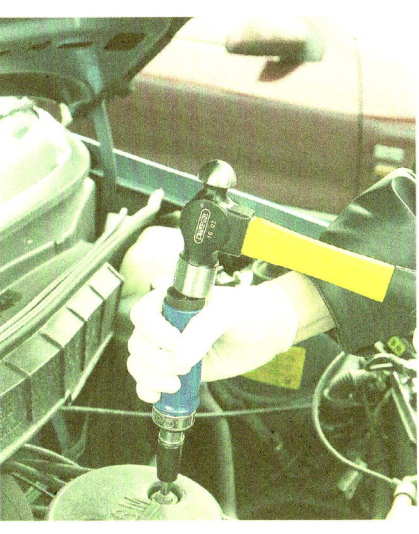

2.4 A good sharp clout with a hammer and well-fitting driver bit will get most stubborn nuts or screws moving. The impact driver works by slightly rotating the bit at the same time as the impact shocks the joint.

HAMMERS

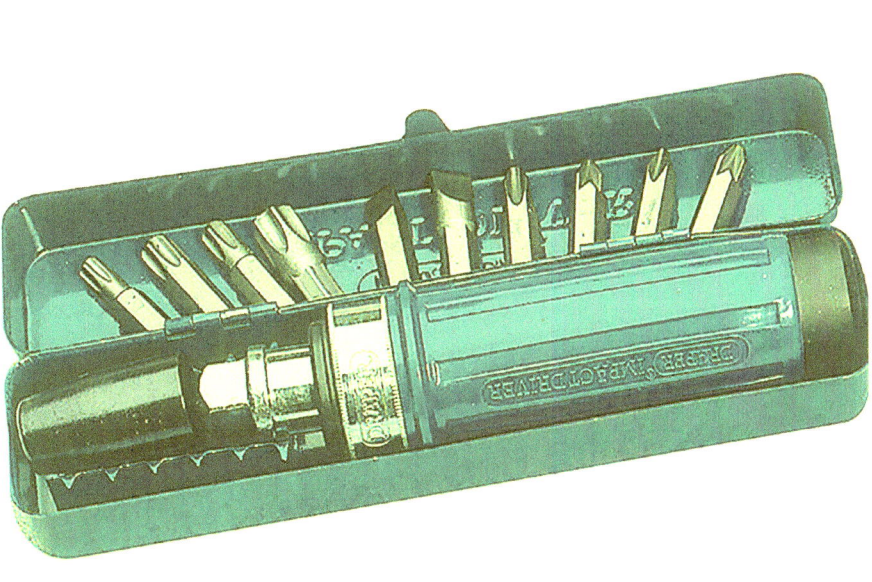

2.3 There will be times when you come across a nut or screw that just will not budge. This is where the impact driver comes in. These are not expensive to buy, and, if used as soon as you know a nut is solid, will save having to drill out a nut or screw that has broken inside the thread. Although you will undoubtedly have one or two that will break off and need drilling out, using an impact driver will keep these to a minimum.

2.5 Use a rubber mallet on softer materials to prevent damage.

CLASSIC MOTORCYCLE RESTORATION

2.6 A good hammer helps with tasks such as knocking out rusted-in spindles, bushes, and shafts, gently easing in or out bolts or bushes, or gently tapping the end of the screwdriver to help split mating surfaces such as casings etc. Fitting tapper bearings to the headstock also requires a firm tap. A rubber hammer is very handy when working with delicate surfaces, too.

CRAFT KNIFE

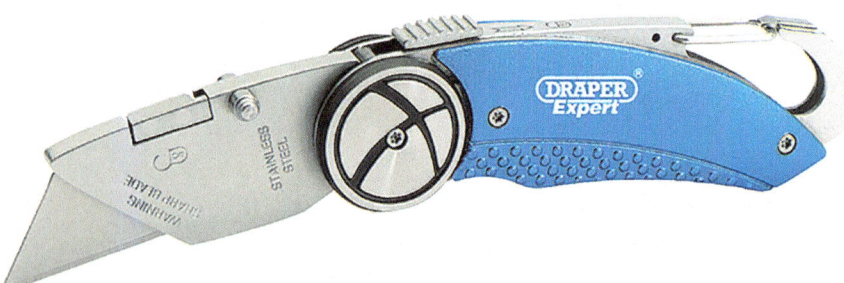

2.7 A sharp Stanley-type knife is used for cutting to size fuel and breather pipe hose, cutting old wires, and trimming gaskets, seat covers, etc.

PLIERS

2.8 A good set of pliers is essential for cutting, squeezing, holding and handling small parts.

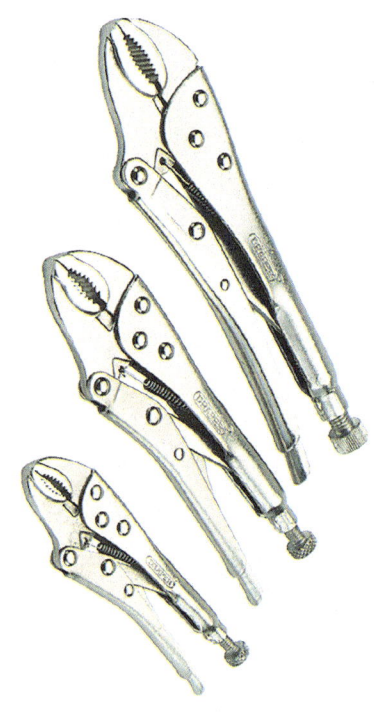

2.9 Mole (vice) grips act like a third hand, and are invaluable when firm clamping is required.

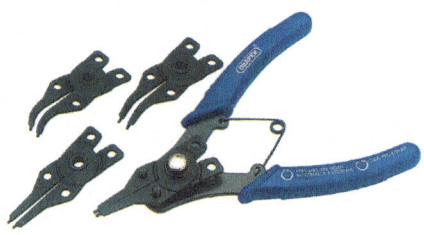

2.10 Circlip pliers are used mainly when dismantling brake and engine components. These are not expensive, and are essential on some occasions.

2.11 If possible, buy separate circlip pliers. These may be more expensive, but are less fiddly and stronger than the universal circlip pliers in the first photo. Remember: circlip pliers come in internal and external types.

TOOLS & EQUIPMENT

2.12 Feeler gauges are used to make very fine adjustments (1000th of an inch, or 10th of a millimetre) in contact breaker points and valve tappets. If you are going to service the engine yourself, these are needed.

TAPS, DIES, DRILLS, AND THREAD REPAIR

Whilst taking apart your project you are likely to come across some troublesome bolts, which can be repaired pretty quickly with the right tools. Taps, dies, drills and thread repair kits come in very handy during a restoration, and are almost certainly going to be needed. If you can get these tools and learn the simple techniques of using them, it will save money by not requiring an engineering shop to carry out the work.

Bolt and stud extractors

These simple tools come in two different forms, and are used to extract broken studs, screws or bolts.

Thread repair kit

Using a thread repair kit is simple: drill out the damaged hole with the drill bit provided, which should be slightly smaller than the hole in question. Next, using the tap provided, cut a new thread, ensuring it is the same size as the original. This will hold the thread insert.

Using the insert tool, screw in the new thread insert. Lastly, snap the small metal tag off the insert by knocking the tool through with a hammer. This will allow the new bolt to pass without obstructions.

2.17 This kit repairs threads that have been stripped through over-tightening, which is common on alloy casings, rocker covers, and heads. The kits include everything needed (from left to right: insert tool, drill bit, tap, and thread inserts) and come in a variety of sizes.

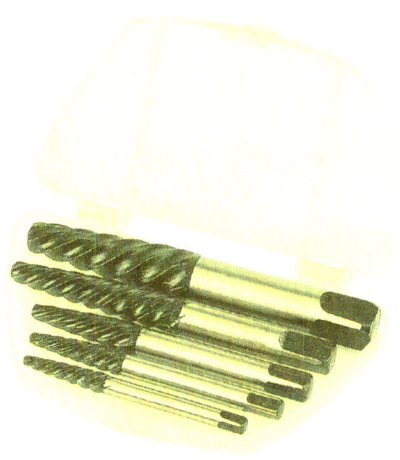

2.15 Simply drill a hole inside the screw or bolt that has broken, and screw one of these extractors in with a socket wrench. The extractor grips the side walls of the broken piece until it moves.

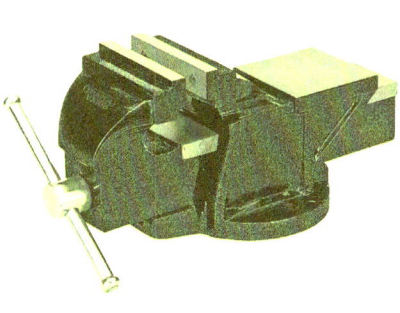

2.13 Wire brushes are used on badly corroded frame parts prior to priming, or on badly rusted bolts to remove rust from the threads. You may not use these very often, but it is handy to have a large and small one in the workshop.

Tap and die set

A tap is slowly turned to cut a thread in a drilled hole. It is important to keep the tap straight, or the screw or bolt that uses the hole will not sit straight. The tap could even break.

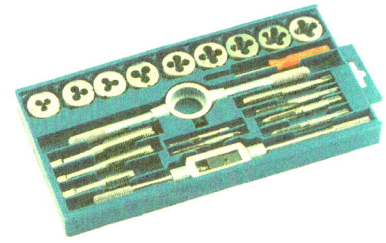

2.18 If you haven't used a tap and die set before, it might be a good idea to practise a couple of times on a piece of scrap metal. It is quite a simple process, and, once mastered, will save you many trips to the engineering workshop.

Important: wear eye protection during this procedure. Rotate the tap about half a turn at a time, backing off after each to help release the swarf (metal cuttings). A little spray of light oil

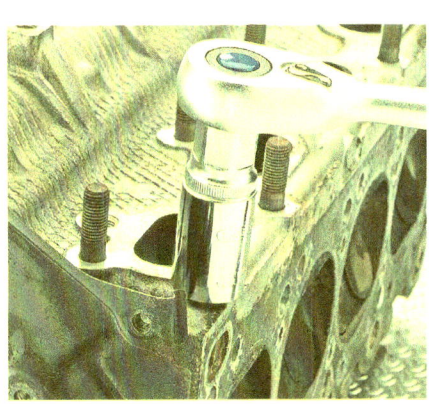

2.14 A bench vice is one of the pieces of equipment I always seem to need. An essential addition to your workshop, useful for many jobs like cutting, polishing, pushing out jammed brake pistons, etc.

2.16 This stud extractor works on exposed bolts, gripping and turning them in an anticlockwise direction until they unscrew.

CLASSIC MOTORCYCLE RESTORATION

will help the tap cut the metal. Slowly keep rotating and backing off half a turn until the thread is cut to the depth that you require. Then unscrew the tap and clean the new thread with a spray of light oil or airline. That's it, you just cut a new thread.

The technique for a die is the same as using the tap. Begin slowly, making half turns, backing off each time and making sure you keep the die straight.

2.19 A brake calliper being re-tapped after the bleed nipple snapped off and had to be drilled out.

2.21 Lastly, drill bits. I am sure you know how to use these. Just remember to always use bits suitable for metal, and wear your goggles.

POWER TOOLS
Pillar drill with vice
Grinder or bench grinder/polisher
Compressor, spray gun
Sonic bath

2.23 Bench grinder/polisher is another very handy tool. Whether sharpening cutting tools for improved work standards and safer use, smoothing burrs and rough edges on cut metals, general metal shaping, or smoothing and polishing, you will soon find the bench grinder necessary for your project. With a polishing kit you can also polish alloy or chrome components to a high standard. Wearing safety goggles is essential when operating a bench grinder.

2.20 A die is the opposite of a tap. It still cuts a new thread, but on a metal rod to make a bolt.

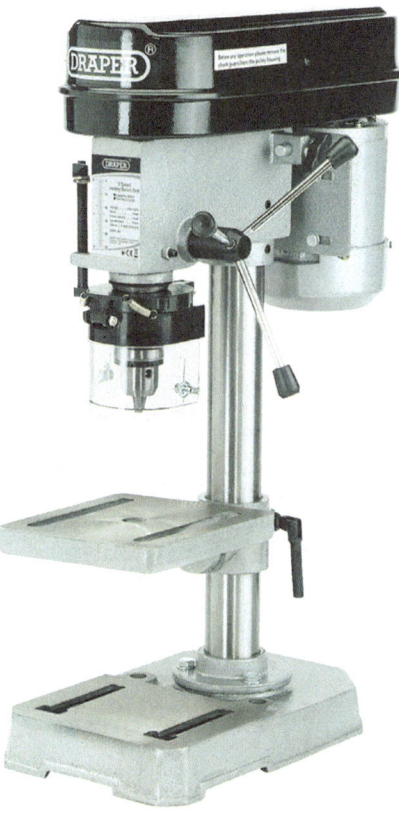

2.22 Although not essential – you could make do with a hand drill – a pillar drill, or drill press as it is also known, is one of the tools that I really wouldn't want to be without. Indispensable for accurate drilling, tasks such as inserting a Heli coil or drilling out a sheared-off bolt are easy to achieve with precise results. Wearing safety goggles is essential when operating a pillar drill.

2.24 If you are going to attempt your own spray work, a good compressor is essential. Small compressors can deplete their air reserve quickly, and take time to build pressure again. Try to get a model that will supply air on demand.

TOOLS & EQUIPMENT

Miscellaneous items

These items are not essential, but will certainly make life easier if you can find it within your budget.

Something to wash parts in – you can buy a dedicated parts washers from tool suppliers. These are great, but an old baby bath or large plastic washing up bowl will do just as well. You will also need a good degreaser and rust remover fluid.

2.25 Commercial parts washers have a built-in pump to deliver degrease fluid over the part being washed, removing dirt and grime in the process. The fluid is recycled through a filter at the bottom, which collects the dirt and rust.

2.27 This lift is smaller, carries less weight, and doesn't lift to the same height as the larger lift. Nevertheless, if you are on a budget, it will still be a useful piece of equipment to have in your workshop, taking the strain off your back.

2.28 GT85 or similar thin lubricating/penetrating oil is a must on any restoration project. It helps release/lubricate rusted parts, and also protects other parts in damp conditions.

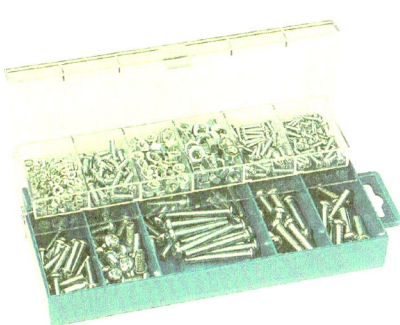

2.26 There are two types of bike lifts. This shows the largest and most desirable. The platform is raised and lowered by an hydraulic pump, similar to a bottle jack.

2.29 A good selection of nuts, bolts and washers will prove invaluable, as many that you remove will be in too poor a condition to re-use. I would use stainless steel if possible, as these will last longer and look better, too.

17

CLASSIC MOTORCYCLE RESTORATION

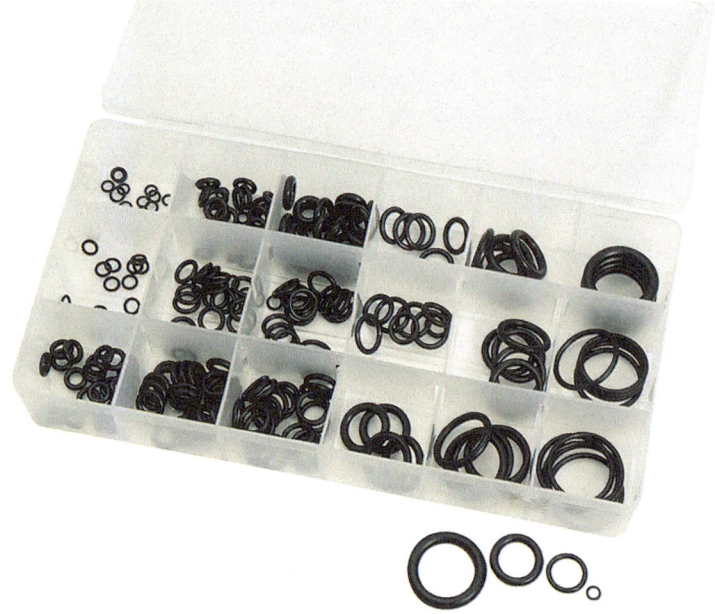

2.30 A box of O ring seals. It's surprising how often these are needed, and they are quite inexpensive when purchased as an assortment.

2.31 Last, but by no means least, try to get a workshop manual specific to your motorcycle as you will need information that this contains. If you're having trouble finding a copy, they can usually be found secondhand on the internet. They provide detailed stripdown and rebuild information for your bike, including torque settings, feeler gauge sizes etc.

Chapter 3
Choosing your first project

Choosing your first project can be quite a task in itself, and depends on things such as budget, your skill level, spares availability, and time.

We all have fond memories of our early days with motorcycles or cars, and it is likely that your first project is a model that you have owned once before and want to ride again, or one you wish you had owned when you were younger. What may have been out of your price range back then may now be in easy reach, if you can just find an example you like.

There are practical matters to consider. For instance, are you the sort of person who would take your motorcycle to the dealer to change a sparkplug, or would you tackle even an engine rebuild yourself? Do you have evenings and weekends free to work on your project, or will you be lucky to grab a spare hour? How much money will you need? This all needs to be thought about before parting with your hard-earned cash.

If you have no experience maintaining a motorcycle or car, it may be easier to buy something less challenging for your first project – maybe one with an engine you can hear running, or that has not been off the road for too long.

You can save a lot of money and time if you can find a part-finished project. For one reason or another some people, despite all their good intentions at the beginning, fail to complete their project. These come up for sale from time to time and could be a great start to restoring a motorcycle.

BUDGET & TIME

Your first project is largely dictated by budget and time. Many enthusiasts like to buy a project that can be completed during the winter months to be ready for the start of the classic bike season, which in the UK is always around Easter time. There are shows and events throughout the year to keeps us all enthusiastic, but the lighter nights and warmer evenings begin to bring us out at Easter and right through the summer months. If you are lucky enough to live in an all-year-round warm climate, we here in the UK envy you. It must be great.

If your other commitments are important, your project could be carried out over a few years, taking the slowly but surely approach. As long as you are enjoying what you are doing, it doesn't matter how long it takes.

If you do decide to carry out a winter project, you really need one that is not going to be too time-consuming, as you only have a few months to get ready for the start of the season. So it would be best to find a project that has good spares availability. Much of the time restoring any motorcycle is spent sourcing parts.

If you buy a rare classic, parts are inevitably also rare, and thus expensive. That odd part you're after is probably wanted by many enthusiasts who have the same project, forcing up the price. On the other hand, if you buy a well-know classic such as a Honda CB400 Four or a Yamaha RD250, you will not have too much trouble finding parts, resulting in the entire project being cheaper in the long run.

We all browse through the classic bike advertisements or the internet and find motorcycles that are in better condition now than when they were first manufactured, and wish we had one just like that. Some become show bikes and are never used on the road at all. The owners of these bikes have spent sometimes thousands on them, and love the thought of making theirs the best of its type. They replace any parts they can with new parts, they have all the chrome replated to a very high standard, and they replace all nuts, bolts and washes with highly

CLASSIC MOTORCYCLE RESTORATION

polished stainless steel. This is a very expensive approach. Please do not look at these bikes and think that we can all achieve this type of finish for a few hundred quid and the occasional hour here and there. This type of restoration can take years.

3.1 A nicely restored Honda CB400F, with a rather interestingly restored BMW in the background, at a bike show in Boston, Lincolnshire.

3.2 An example of an aftermarket indicator. Identical to the original, but not always liked by purists.

Spares availability should be high on your priority list when you choose your project bike. Many early Japanese motorcycles shared parts with other bikes from the same manufacturer. This is a great help, as long as you know which model has the same parts as your bike.

Throughout this book are photos of a 1973 Honda CB350 Four that I restored. This is a good example of parts sharing by a manufacturer. Even though this motorcycle was never sold in the UK, it has been a good project, simply because of the amount of parts it shares with other models. If new parts were no longer available, I used parts from the CB400 Four, but also the 500, 550, 750 four, along with the CB350 twin etc.

Lights, indicators, switches, clocks, and some chrome parts are interchangeable on many motorcycles. This gives you a much better chance of finding a good condition used part if originals are no longer available.

There are many aftermarket replica parts available. Some restorers do not like to use non-original parts; others do not mind so much. If you intend to enter your finished motorcycle in shows, you really need original parts to compete. On the other hand, if you are happy that your bike

3.3 A classic example of a basket case. Many parts are missing. A good example of what not to buy.

looks as near 100% original as you can get it, there are some very good replica parts available that look almost identical to the original.

There are many 'projects' for sale that are far from complete, or are really just a large collection of spare parts. This is an expensive way to begin. It is always best to buy a complete bike for your first project. You can strip it

down at your own pace, learning how it comes apart and how it eventually goes back together. You can examine each part you remove, and decide if that part is re-useable or needs work.

Parts such as rubbers and odd-shaped bolts always seem to be missing when you buy an incomplete project. These are difficult to get hold of, because they are small and do not

CHOOSING YOUR FIRST PROJECT

have much value. They are not often seen for sale, but you can't put your bike back together without them.

There are always exceptions to rules, if you are brave. In this case the exception would be if you are lucky enough to come across a rare classic that, once restored, would be a real collector's piece – maybe a BSA Gold Star or an early Kawasaki Z900. Then it may be worth considering a box of bits, but this is not for the faint-hearted, and is not a cheap or quick project.

IMPORTED PROJECTS

Once you know your budget and limitations, you can begin to concentrate on finding the right bike for you. The choice is endless, and one area worth considering is the imported motorcycle market. There is a larger selection of models available in the USA and Japan, with many more early Japanese models than we can find here in the UK. These can be real bargains, and are often in very good condition for their age, frequently coming from a warmer climate.

There is nothing wrong with taking on such a project, as long as you know what you are letting yourself in for. Many are sold unrestored and unregistered. This in itself isn't a big problem, but does involve more time and paperwork.

Firstly, it is very important that the seller has the original import documents. This shows that the correct import duty and tax has been paid. If this is not available, I would look for another project. If the documents are not in order you will have difficulty registering the finished bike with the relevant authorities. If the documents are in order, this is the current procedure to register an imported motorcycle (or car) in the UK:

Any imported motorcycle that needs to be registered requires a current MoT certificate. The MoT station issues the certificate with the frame number of the motorcycle on it, as you won't have a registration number yet.

You also need a current insurance policy. Your insurance company can issue you a cover note with the chassis/frame number on. This is because, as with the MoT, at this stage you won't have a registration number.

3.4 A typical USA import needing restoration – coming from a warm climate, the chrome is in very good original condition.

The cover note and MoT certificate allow you to register and tax the motorcycle. The cover note usually lasts for 30 days, giving you time to apply for your V5 document. Once registered, call the insurance company and tell it the age-related registration number that the DVLA has issued you.

If your motorcycle has never been registered in the UK before, your local DVLA office usually asks to see your motorcycle before issuing a V5 document and tax disc. This is to check that the details you have given on the registration application form are correct.

If you are importing a motorcycle into a country other than the UK, check the import regulations for your country.

DIFFERENT TYPES OF PROJECTS

There are several types of project you may wish to consider. If you attend any classic motorcycle show, you will see bikes that have been restored beyond their original specification and design. Many have highly polished alloy and chrome, and also crazy, even beautiful paintwork. You will see motorcycles that have been restored as a café racer or race replica, and also the special, a bike made of parts from completely different manufacturers. Here are a few examples.

The original restoration

3.5 A nicely restored, 1973 Honda CB350 Four: unusual in the UK, and looking very much as it would when new. The exhausts are not original, but the builder has stayed with the 4-into-4 exhaust system, as Honda designed it. The colours and decals are original.

3.6 A better-than-new looking 1976 Suzuki AP50. Note the pedals – it's a moped!

CLASSIC MOTORCYCLE RESTORATION

The show restoration

3.7 Here is a very smart, show-winning, Yamaha 350LC. This far exceeds what a 350LC would have looked like when it was new, and gives a good example of the standard you need to reach should you decide to restore a motorcycle to enter into shows. Custom paintwork, aftermarket parts, and attention to every detail are the order of the day here.

The café racer

Many restorers build bikes to the café racer style to replicate the race bikes of the past. Some are registered for the road, and many are brought to track day events, allowing the owner to show them off, and even ride them to their full potential.

The special

In the 1950s/'60s, motorcycle enthusiasts knew that the Norton featherbed frame was the best available. However, they also knew that the Vincent engines produced the best power. This led to enthusiasts using the Vincent engines in the Norton frames, a combination that became known as 'the Norvin.' There were many other combinations, such as the TriBsa, and even the Norton Imp – a Hillman Imp car engine fitted into a Norton frame.

3.9 BSA never made a 4-cylinder motorcycle, but here is one that has been built by the owner. A good example of marrying parts from more than one manufacturer.

CHECK LIST

Many of the faults here are not uncommon on projects, and you shouldn't be too afraid if your bike has some of these defects – after all, it is a restoration. Knowing what to look out for will help you decide whether this is the right project for you, and will serve as a bargaining tool when haggling with the seller.

All projects were someone's pride and joy at one time. Over the years they suffer from poor maintenance and become neglected. If the previous owner didn't know how to maintain a bike properly, it could have been something as simple as a bad set of contact points or a broken cable that stopped it running, and the owner, not knowing how to resolve the problem, never used it again. Assess what the original problem was, and fix it during your restoration.

Once the bike has been left standing, parts begin to seize and rubbers begin to crack, and the chrome and alloy oxidise. To bring your project back to its former glory all these problems need to be resolved.

3.8 This is an example of a café racer. It looks so good it could even be an original racing bike.

CHOOSING YOUR FIRST PROJECT

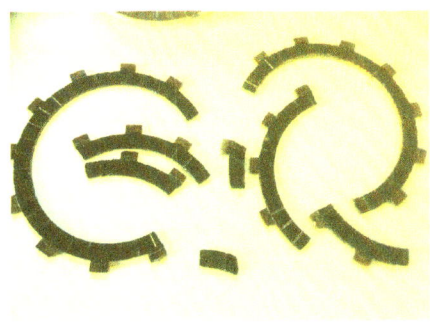

3.10 Clutch plates discovered on my latest project.

Here are things to look out for, and also a checklist for when you first view your project. All problems can be overcome, but the worse the problem, the more expensive it is to fix.

First impressions

Begin with your overall first impression of the motorcycle. Is it all there? Are there obviously parts missing? Side covers, indicator lenses, levers and lights are common missing parts.

Does the owner have the keys? If they do not have the keys and you cannot get the original keys made, you will need to buy a complete set of locks.

Do the engine and frame numbers match? The engine may have been changed at one time, and purists frown on a motorcycle that does not have the original. Not everyone is so bothered, but it is worth keeping in mind.

Are the V5 documents present? Having them will save time when taxing the bike.

Does the owner have any old manuals? Many do, and it will really help if you are given them on purchasing the bike.

Are there any spare parts? Many owners have a box full of bits they think are worthless. Take them if they are available. Often you will find a part that you need later on.

Does it look like someone just stopped using it and left it as it was, or does it look like someone has tinkered with it? Giveaway signs are screws not put back, and side panels and battery missing.

The engine

Let's begin with the engine. If it starts and runs, fine. Look out for excessive smoke, rattles, etc. If it's a 2-stroke it will smoke on start-up and clear a little after a few minutes, which is normal. This is how the pistons and other parts are lubricated when the engine is running.

If it is a 4-stroke it should hardly smoke at all. On first starting it will be rich with the choke on, and may look a little smoky until warmed up, after which there should be none. Don't confuse smoke with steam. If a bike had been unused for some time moisture can build up in the exhaust, and when restarted this turns to steam, which can be confused with smoke. Smoke is darker with a more oily smell.

Are there any unusual noises? Listen out for internal knocking or rattles. If you are unfamiliar with how an engine should sound, take a more experienced friend with you.

If the engine does not start

Does the engine turn over? Try the kickstart to check. (If it has an electric starter, it is unlikely that there is any life in the battery.) This will tell you if the engine is seized. If it is, it could be expensive to resolve.

3.12 This piston was so seized it had to be drilled and hammered out! The damage to the cylinder bore led to a complete rebore.

Can you pull in the clutch lever and open the throttle smoothly? This will give you an idea of how long a bike has been standing. These things take a long time to seize, and if they are

3.11 Does the engine have all the sparkplugs in place? Absent sparkplugs are not a good sign, especially if the bike is stored outside, as moisture will have got in and caused cylinder damage. I had to buy a complete cylinder head for a motorcycle once, due to water ingress.

CLASSIC MOTORCYCLE RESTORATION

stuck it is another problem that needs solving.

Can you select all the gears? Try rocking the bike backwards and forward while moving the gearlever to select all the gears. You may need help with this if the bike is heavy.

The tank and seat

With many classic bikes it is hard to find a secondhand fuel tank, and those that are available have a high asking price. Most are not available new, and aftermarket fuel tanks are not usually made (there are a few about though).

Take a good look at the tank. The cosmetics can be overcome, but it is holes that we are really looking out for.

3.14 The overall shape of this tank is good, and it can be resprayed. Measure the position of the stripes, so that, once it has been resprayed, you know exactly where to place them.

3.13 Take off the fuel cap and have a good look inside. Is it clean or dirty? If dirty, how bad is it? If the tank has a hole in it like the one pictured, a replacement is likely to be needed. When viewing the bike with the fuel cap on, this tank looked okay!

Does the tank hold its original shape? No bad dents or damage? Although such things can be overcome, the worse it is, the more expensive it is to repair.

Most classic bikes had metal seat bases that rust. A little rust can be dealt with, but a badly rotted base will need changing, if you can find a replacement. Seat covers from most classic bikes are easily available, but if the seat base has rotted there is nothing to attach a cover to, and the hinges will likely be loose so you could also have a problem securing the seat to the frame.

Foam is not such a problem, but good foam is a great advantage.

3.15 The seat will almost certainly need attention. It is not often you find a seat cover still intact, but aesthetics are easily improved with a new one. Ensure that the frame and seat base are good quality. This is a good condition seat base, with firm hinges and only light rust. All the seat rubbers are still in place.

Cutting foam to shape is an art, and not easy to get right.

Frame and forks

Look for obvious damage to the frame and forks. Many bikes have been 'dropped' in their lifetime, and any heavily accident-damaged bike should be avoided. Look out for bent forks, swinging arm, stands, footrests, gear and brake levers, and dents and deep scratches.

CHOOSING YOUR FIRST PROJECT

3.16 This seat cover and trim have seen better days, although the foam was still useable.

If they are rusted, it is likely they need re-chroming. Some light rust can polish out, but anything worse than this leads to leaking oil seals. This is not uncommon, and in most cases the oil seals would be changed during a restoration.

It is normal for a bike that has been standing for some time to be low, if not empty of fork oil. Push the forks down and let go – do they bounce up and down quickly? It shows that the damping has been lost, and it's likely that the seals will need replacing and the forks refilling with fork oil. The oil dampens the movement, so there should be very little bounce.

3.17 These forks are showing some signs of slight pitting on the stanchions. If the pitting is not within the lower fork leg range of movement, it is possible to leave regrinding until a later date. However, it is recommended that the fork legs be re-chromed if possible. The ones here need a good polish, too.

Take a look head-on and from behind the bike to see if it looks square and symmetrical. Footrests should be the same height and level. Look at the exhaust pipes – these are the first part of the bike to be damaged in a fall, but can easily be replaced to conceal accidents.

The forks should be 100% straight. It is an expensive job to replace stanchions and fork legs. Make sure you look at them and compare them with each other. Check carefully that they are not bent.

The forks may be twisted in the top and bottom yoke, but do not confuse this with them being bent. Forks that are twisted can easily be reset by loosening the top and bottom yoke bolts and pulling the forks straight.

Take a look at the fork stanchions.

Chapter 4
Sourcing parts

Once you have bought your first project and begun the initial stripdown, you soon build a large shopping list of parts required, which only grows the further you get into the restoration. So where do you get all those elusive parts from?

THE INTERNET
The internet is undoubtedly the best place to begin looking. Auction websites have thousands of parts advertised from all over the world. On websites such as eBay, you can often find half a dozen vendors selling the parts that you are looking for, many of which can be delivered to your door in a few days. You often see close-up images of the part for sale, giving a good indication of condition. On the other hand, you can sometimes find vague descriptions and blurry images that don't describe the part properly. Be careful about purchasing these.

eBay rules at the moment are that, if you buy something on auction (rather than 'Buy It Now'), you have no right to a refund if you change your mind after the purchase, unless it was not as described by the seller. If the item you bought was a 'Buy It Now' instant purchase, then you have the option to ask the seller for a full refund if you find the part unsuitable. This usually includes postage costs, too. Check eBay's returns policy for more details.

Be aware that if you buy a part from an international seller, it's possible that, when it arrives in your country, you could be charged a customs duty charge, and maybe a tax charge, too. All countries have different import rules, and you should check yours before buying from an international seller. Importing parts is often a good – if not the only – option, and extra charges are not always a deal breaker.

The downside of buying from an internet seller is that, at the time of purchase, you cannot see the item you are buying in detail, and have to wait for delivery before you can make a true assessment of its condition.

I live in the UK, and have purchased parts from the USA, Germany, France, Japan, and Hong Kong, and have always been happy with what I have bought.

CLUBS AND FORUMS
The benefits of joining a club or forum cannot be stressed enough. They are a great way to source parts, and by joining you will get to know the best, most recommended sources for your bike.

Many club members are marque specialists, who have owned and worked on their type of bike for years. They know every single model and part in extreme detail, and give valuable advice to new members – not only on sourcing parts, but also on fault diagnosis, and explaining the easiest way to overcome problems that may seem difficult to a beginner. You can be sure that some members have come across the same problems you are likely to face, and will already know the simplest solution. Later in the book I list clubs and forums for different marques.

A Suzuki GT750 forum I visit has the following sections:

Faults and cures
Stock faults and cures
Meetings and events
GT250, 380, 550 and GT500 section [all these bikes have something in common with the 750]
Your restoration stories
Buy, sell, exchange
Recommended services
Where's my old bike?
Like-for-like items and good value eBay items
Reference pictures of restored bikes and technical bulletins
Specials modifications and street

SOURCING PARTS

fighter track day bikes
General chat

You can see by this list that there is very little, if anything, that is not included. The references and tech help posts are very good, and the advice given will save you time and money. There are forums and clubs for almost every motorcycle, and for more common motorcycles there are often several clubs or forums that would suit your needs.

Some forums and clubs even have parts that are no longer available from the manufacturer remade themselves. If there is enough demand, someone will find a way to make the part.

Many other specialist websites also sell parts for classic bikes and carry out repairs, too.

MAGAZINES

Magazines should not be overlooked. At the time of writing there were at least eight classic bike monthly magazines on sale in the UK, most also sold internationally. They all have a classified advert section at the back, including handfuls of classic bike dealers with parts for sale. This remains a good source of parts, and buying specialist magazines can also put you in touch with experts such as engine rebuilders, chrome platers, sprayers, powder coating companies and the like.

THE AUTO JUMBLE

The auto jumble – or swap meet – is my favourite way of sourcing parts. Imagine a market full of stalls selling bikes, parts and accessories just for classics, with thousands of other enthusiasts sorting through boxes looking for the last little part to finish their project.

Although they can be more time consuming, at an auto jumble you can see the parts on sale close-up, can haggle with the seller, and can take the part away with you that day. Often the seller will be able to advise you on other parts you may need, or other parts they have at home that are also for sale.

4.1 A typical stall at an auto jumble will be full of interesting parts for sale.

4.0 Magazines have stories about others who have restored bikes. There are technical articles, and venues and dates for upcoming events such as auto jumbles, classic bike shows, and race meetings.

It is not only parts for sale, but bikes, too. Some look like they have just been dragged out of the local river, and others are in immaculate condition. Many dealers focus on a particular manufacturer or model, while others will have a mix and match approach. Lots of the stalls holders are traders who sell parts and bikes for a living, others have small stalls and are maybe just selling parts from old projects they have accumulated over the years. Either way, in my opinion, this is the most enjoyable way to source parts. I arrange to meet up with my friends, I look out for what they are after, and vice versa. Refreshments are always available, and you can have a good day out enjoying your hobby. At the end of the day I load up the car with all the goodies I've bought, feeling satisfied that I have some extra parts to go towards finishing my latest project. I'm not always lucky finding what I

CLASSIC MOTORCYCLE RESTORATION

4.2 A nice selection of old Hondas being inspected by potential buyers.

need, but it is always an enjoyable day. Believe me, you never take enough money. Every stall seems to have something you would like to buy, and there is always that other potential project to be seen.

Many sellers at auto jumbles have traded like this for years, and are knowledgeable and reasonable with their prices. It is not only used and old parts for sale – you can find stalls selling new fuel pipes, nuts and bolts, badges, stickers ... the list goes on.

Many auto jumbles are simply an auto market with parts and bikes for sale, but others are part of a much bigger classic bike show, such as those at the Stafford show ground and Newark.

I am sure you will find what you need using these sources, and will have your project finished in no time!

4.3 11,000 people arrived on a freezing January weekend at a classic bike show in Newark, hoping to find the parts they were looking for.

Chapter 5
Getting started

Begin the initial stripdown by assessing the condition of the engine. Providing that you can get it running at this stage and all seems okay, it will simply be a case of cleaning and polishing it before putting it back in the frame.

CAUTION! Before you do anything with the engine, check the oil and water levels, and top up if necessary. Don't get caught out trying to start the engine only to discover the oil leaked out years ago. Damage caused to the engine when run with no oil will undoubtedly lead to an expensive repair bill, which can easily be avoided.

We begin with the basic checks on the ignition and fuel system.

Try turning the key in the ignition. Usually some oil or neutral lights will come on, but not always.

Give a good kick on the kickstarter, or a quick press on the electric start, whilst having a close look at the sparkplug electrode. Does it spark? This is what you are looking for. If it sparks, great – you are in business and the ignition side is looking okay. Do the same check on the other sparkplugs if you have a multi-cylinder engine. If any of your plugs don't give a spark, it could be a faulty cap or plug.

5.0 On all my restoration projects I have always purchased a new battery. A good quality motorbike battery will last years, and, at this stage, if you cannot start the bike, it could save you endless hours investigating why. Get a good quality battery, and install it in the battery compartment.

You can investigate properly later.

Having checked your sparkplugs, next check the fuel system. We will assume the fuel tank is clean. Put in some fresh fuel, pull the fuel hose from the carburettor, turn on the fuel tap, and see if there is any fuel coming out. Do this only briefly to assess whether you have a clear tap.

Turn the fuel tap to the 'off' position, and unscrew and remove the

5.1 Take out one of the sparkplugs and lay it on the cylinder head. Do NOT hold the sparkplug! Hold the plug cap, otherwise you are likely to get a shock – this is how I found out my electrics were okay on my very first project, to the great amusement of my friends.

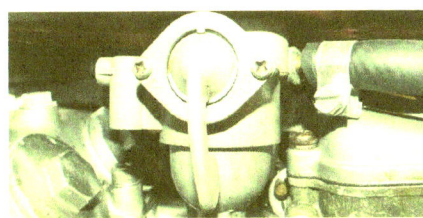

5.2 Fuel taps generally have a small filter inside that is easily blocked. If there is fuel coming out, turn off the tap and reconnect the fuel hose to the carburettor. This is a Honda fuel tap in the 'on' position: also showing 'stop' and 'reserve.'

CLASSIC MOTORCYCLE RESTORATION

fuel pipe, ready to remove the tank later. Drain the fuel from the tank into a suitable container.

Once you know the ignition and the fuel side are okay, attempt to start the engine. Do this in an open space – not inside a garage or shed – because the exhaust gases are dangerous if breathed in.

If the engine starts, let it warm up. The engine may not have been started for years, so don't rev it too much. Listen for any strange noises, and look for oil and water leaks.

If there are no obvious problems, assume the engine is okay. If, after going through the basic starting check, the engine does not start you need to investigate later.

Once you have assessed whether or not the engine is good, move to the next stage of the stripdown.

STARTING THE STRIPDOWN

It is a good practice to make a photographic record of the motorcycle and its parts as you are stripping it. You can refer back to it when putting all the parts back together.

5.3 Begin by spraying nuts, bolts, or screws with a light oil such as GT85, to begin penetrating and help free any stuck parts.

You will find your impact driver very useful here, particularly on engine casing screws. Ensure you use the correct size spanner, socket, or screwdriver the first time you attempt to undo something – all too often people try to undo a screw or nut with the wrong-sized tool, resulting in it becoming rounded and even more difficult to release. There are tools such as bolt extractors if this happens, but it is far better to remove the item correctly to begin with. Some will be very stubborn, and may require a firm clout with the impact wrench, or warming with a blow lamp.

5.4 Hold the impact wrench firmly on the nut or in the screw, so that it does not bounce out when striking it. Hit the wrench with a club hammer – this will give the turning action that you need, alongside the impact to crack the seal of the seized bolt or nut. Often it is not the thread that is stuck, but the head of the nut or screw. I sometimes give casing screws a light sideways tap to help break the seal between them and the casing, always being careful not to damage the casing itself.

5.5 With nuts such as those on engine mounting bolts, use a good socket and hold the other end of the bolt firmly with a suitable size spanner to prevent it turning. Usually, once the nut begins to move, it will quickly become loose. If it stays very tight, spray on more light oil as more thread becomes visible. This will also help when it comes to the rebuild.

GETTING STARTED

Begin removing the larger parts of the bike so you can access other parts. Remove the seat and tank.

The fuel tank will be held in place by either a bolt or a rubber strap.

5.6 Try to organize bolts and screws into containers and keep them grouped. I place all the engine mounting bolts in one container, separate from other bolts of a similar size. Label all the containers.

5.9 The tank clip is on a rubber quick release strap on this example, and just requires pulling off the tank locating hooks.

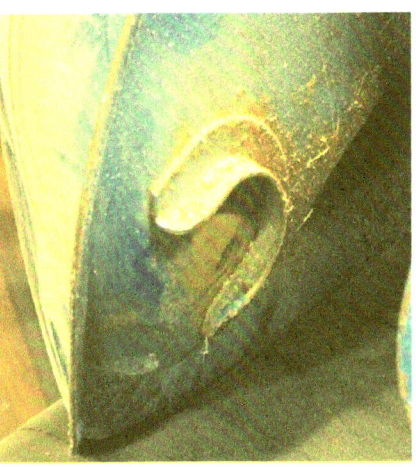

5.12 The front of the fuel tank has two brackets that locate onto the fuel tank rubbers.

5.7 The seat will usually be held by two seat pins that have a split pin in the end. Pull out the pin and store safely – you will need it later.

5.10 Most fuel tanks have a bolt securing the rear.

5.13 The fuel tank rubbers attached to the frame reduce vibration to the tank. If these are in poor condition, they should be replaced.

5.8 Remove the seat pin. This should pull out quite easily, but, if it doesn't, give it a tap on the end using a small screwdriver and light hammer to push it out.

5.11 Simply pull the tank backward and up a little to free it from the locating rubbers that are hidden under the front of the fuel tank.

31

CLASSIC MOTORCYCLE RESTORATION

Next, begin removing the side panels, lights, indicators, and cables. Try not to damage any electrical connections – always pull the connector, not the wire itself. Remove the entire electrical loom and the cables. The cables may be serviceable, and if they look okay it is worth lubricating them with some light oil, as this will help you later.

REMOVING THE ENGINE

The following procedure describes the basics of removing the engine. You will find more detailed instructions in your model specific workshop manual. Unless you have an engine lift, you will need someone else to help you with lifting.

5.14 Do not pull the wires, as they may come loose. Pull the connector plug instead.

5.18 Remove the split link from the drive chain as shown. By squeezing hard on the split link, it should pop off from the chain link. If this proves difficult, you can prise it off with a screwdriver.

5.15 Unscrew the side panels from below.

5.19 Disconnect and remove all air filters.

5.16 Most side panels have two slots that hook onto the frame. Once the screw underneath is removed, the side panel can be lifted off.

5.17 When the seat and tank are removed, you will be able to see the condition of the wiring, rubbers, and other parts that were covered.

5.20 Remove all carburettors.

GETTING STARTED

5.21 To remove the carburettors, withdraw the carburettor slides. On most models it is simply a case of unscrewing the top and pulling it free.

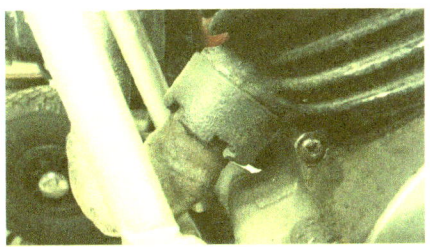

5.22 Unscrew all exhaust manifolds. This is a screw-on type, but often these are also held in with two bolts. Next, remove the complete exhaust system.

IMPORTANT! The engine is very heavy, so a suitable engine lift is needed. In the absence of such, always ask for assistance when lifting it out of the frame. Never attempt it on your own!

5.25 Once the engine mounting bolts have been removed, the engine can be lifted and placed on a strong bench for inspection later.

5.23 There are usually three or four engine mounting bolts. Use two spanners to prevent the bolt moving while undoing it.

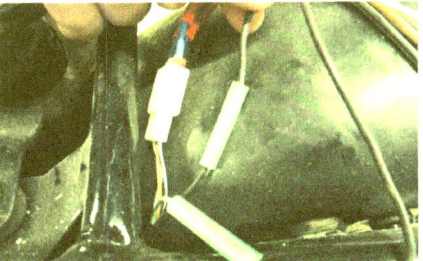

5.26 Disconnect all remaining wires that are attached to the lights and indicators.

5.28 Check the lenses, cables, and chrome work, and decide whether the indicators are in good enough condition to be re-used later. Also check the reflectors, if fitted.

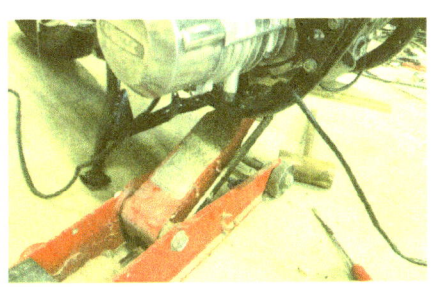

5.24 Support the engine with a suitable jack and a piece of wood before removing the engine mounting bolts.

5.27 Unscrew the nuts holding the indicators in place. Some screw into the frame and have a locking nut, others screw right through the frame and have a nut and washer on the other end.

5.29 The chrome is often in poor condition, but indicator stems can usually be bought separately.

CLASSIC MOTORCYCLE RESTORATION

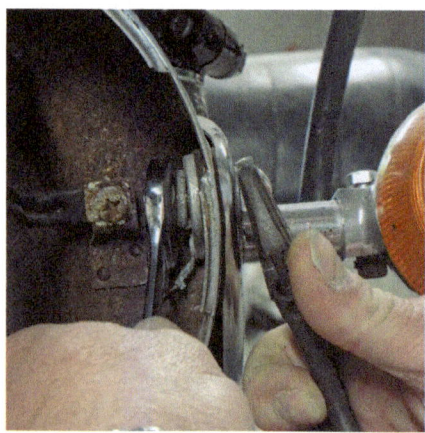

5.30 When unbolting the headlamp, hold the bolt with two spanners to prevent it turning.

5.33 Those mudguards with stays have an additional four bolts lower down the fork leg.

5.34 Some motorcycles have a plastic inner mudguard, which simply pulls out.

5.31 Four bolts hold on the rear mudguard, and each has a metal sleeve and rubber. Disconnect the wires, then unscrew all the bolts and remove the mudguard.

5.35 Remove all the smaller parts, and keep together for cleaning later.

5.36 Somewhere in here are the connectors for the handlebar switchgear. Disconnect all connectors now, and thread through the rear of the headlamp bowl.

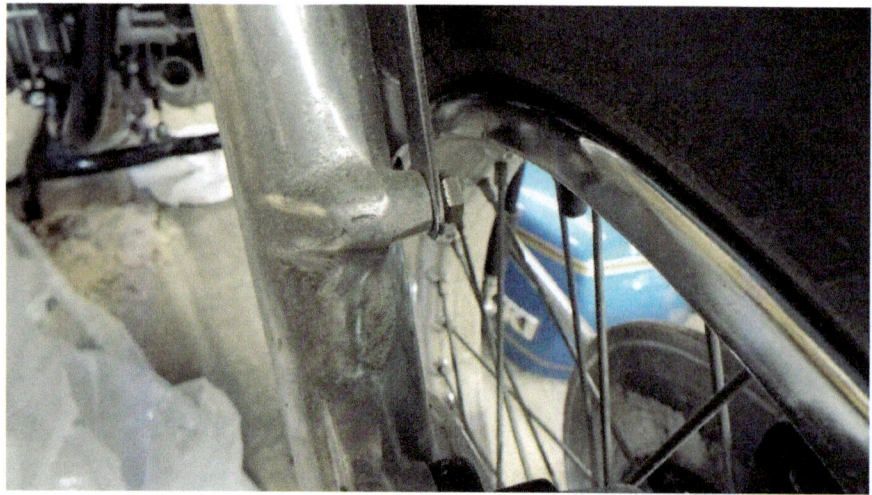

5.37 Now remove the complete loom. In this case there were so many bad repairs that it was necessary to purchase a new one.

5.32 There are two bolts in each fork leg supporting the front mudguard.

GETTING STARTED

5.38 Remove the switchgear by undoing the screws underneath.

5.39 Unscrew the four handlebar bolts and remove the handlebars.

Now all you should have is a rolling chassis – just wheels and a frame. Find something to support the frame underneath the engine compartment, just like you did when removing the engine, because you will soon be removing the wheels, forks, swinging arm, and stands. This is much easier if the frame is supported. I use a small axle stand.

Once the frame is supported remove the wheels, then the forks, main and sidestand, and swinging arm. This will leave you with only the frame. Remember to put the castle nuts with split pins back on the wheel spindles for safekeeping.

5.40 Loosen the two rear wheel adjusters, and remove the rear wheel spindle too. All castle nuts should have a split pin. If any are missing, buy some for your rebuild.

5.41 Remove the castle nut seen in photo 5.23, and withdraw the front wheel spindle.

35

CLASSIC MOTORCYCLE RESTORATION

5.42 Unscrew and withdraw the swinging arm bolt – a small one is shown here (there is a larger one in photo 5.5). You will probably need to tap this out with a hammer and long slim bar or similar.

5.44 and 5.45 There are two pinch bolts holding each fork in place: one at the top and one at the bottom. Loosen these, but be prepared for the fork to slip down. Often the forks need a gentle tap with a mallet at the top to start them moving. Remove the forks completely now.

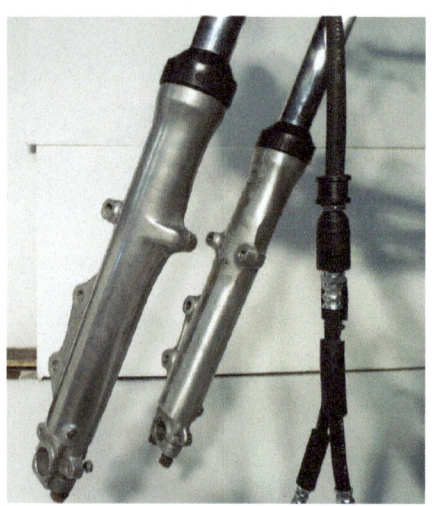

5.43 The forks with front wheel removed.

TIP! When dismantling the bike, it is a good practice to put the screws and bolts back in the hole they came out of. Not only you will not lose any parts, you always know where they came from. You can always put in a newer one later, but this way you will always know the correct size and type of screw/bolt that came out. Also, try to group nuts and bolts. For instance, keep all the engine mounting bolts, washers and nuts together in a small box, and label it.

Put both stands, swinging arm and frame on one side, these will all be powder-coated or sprayed. Be sure to

5.46 With everything now removed from the frame we will now need to look for any cracked welds or other damage.

GETTING STARTED

5.47 This frame was cleaned with a pressure washer to remove all dirt and grime.

Once everything is degreased you need to flatten any old scratches or chip marks.

5.49 You will need a selection of different grades of wet and dry paper.

remove the old swinging arm bushes before spraying. If you have any other metal items, these can be done at the same time.

If you have decided to have your frame powder-coated, now is the time to send off these parts.

If you are going to spray the larger items they now need to be prepared. Begin by degreasing with your degreaser and a small brush, carefully checking for any cracks in the frame. These will need welding/brazing if you find any damage.

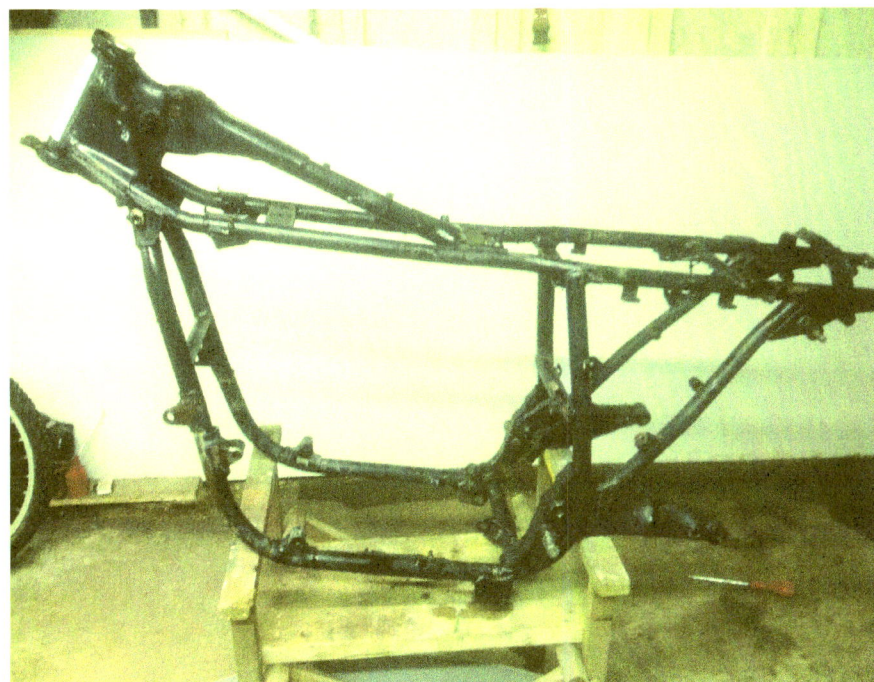

5.48 The frame has now been degreased and dried, awaiting preparation.

5.50 Begin with around 120 grade coarse paper to remove the worst of the rust.

5.51 Go over again with a finer grade such as 240. Ensure the frame is well-supported – it is heavy.

37

CLASSIC MOTORCYCLE RESTORATION

5.52 A multitool will save time and is great for sanding those awkward areas. Remove all old stickers at this stage.

Apply tape to protect areas you do not want painted: from the connecting areas to the swinging bushes. Insert screws in any threads that you do not want paint to get into.

When spraying, be sure to wear the appropriate protective mask and clothing, as the fumes are toxic.

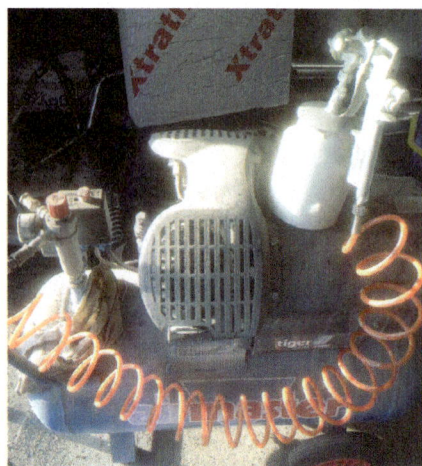

5.53 A good capacity compressor and spray gun setup is needed if you intend to do the spraying yourself.

5.54 If you don't have spraying equipment, good results can still be achieved with spray cans. In the case of Hammerite no priming is necessary, and only two coats of the finish gloss are required.

GETTING STARTED

5.55 Now spray the entire frame with two coats of primer. Patience is the key with spraying, so ensure each coat is 100% dry before applying the finishing coats.

5.57 Complete frame after two coats of primer.

5.58 Apply two coats of the finish gloss. At this stage go over the entire frame (or the most visible areas if you want to save some time) with a very fine wet and dry paper, such as 800-1000 grade. By doing this you will get a much shinier gloss finish.

5.56 Suspending smaller parts makes it easier to spray all sides without having to touch or move the part.

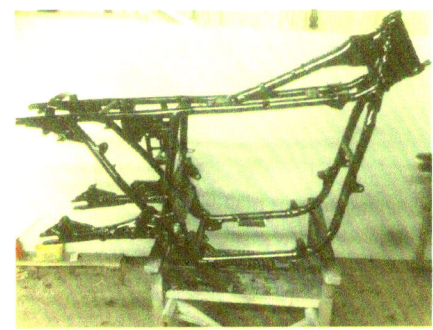

5.59 Spray all black items at the same time. This includes the swinging arm and stands, and can also include engine mounting brackets, the electrical backplate, and the air filter housing.

The frame is now finished and ready for your rebuild.

39

Chapter 6
Cleaning & polishing

Now that you have a newly-painted or powder-coated frame, it's time to turn your attention to the other parts of your motorcycle. Each item must be cleaned and polished to bring it up to the best possible finish. Many parts may be too rusty or damaged to salvage, or may need sending off for chrome plating.

Begin with a thorough cleaning of each part. This allows you to assess the condition, guarantee good working order of all components that may be clogged with years of dust and dirt, and ensure good paint adhesion for the parts to be painted and sprayed.

SAFETY TIPS BEFORE YOU BEGIN

Always use safety equipment. Wear a dust mask, safety goggles, and gloves at all times.

Always apply the item being finished to the area of the polishing mop that is rotating away from you.

Cover and tie long hair to prevent entanglement with machines.

Fasten loose cuffs and loose clothing. Remove or secure long necklaces to prevent entanglement.

If the polishing wheel 'grabs' the item being polished, let it go – do not hold on.

DEGREASING

Engine and frame parts will need to be degreased with a suitable agent. Smaller parts can be placed in a bucket and cleaned with a small paint brush, while larger parts, such as the frame, need to be cleaned in an area that will suffer least from the mess caused. Standing a frame on its end in a large plastic container, such as an old baby bath, and leaning it against a wall works well, and keeps the dirt contained. Degreaser also has to be rinsed off, and the parts dried as soon as possible. This is particularly important with ferrous parts, which quickly rust again if not dried and protected appropriately.

ULTRASONIC CLEANING

An ultrasonic cleaner uses ultrasound vibrations and an appropriate cleaning solvent (sometimes ordinary tap water) to clean small or delicate items. Many larger cleaners have a temperature control right up to 80c. The combination of ultrasonic vibrations of around 23,000kHz and heat make a very good cleaning force. Originally used to sterilise surgical instruments, these machines are now available to buy at reasonable prices. The sizes are given in the amount of liquid they can hold, and the dimensions of the basket the parts are held in.

6.1 A free-standing parts washer can be very useful, if your budget will stretch to one.

CLEANING & POLISHING

EQUIPMENT

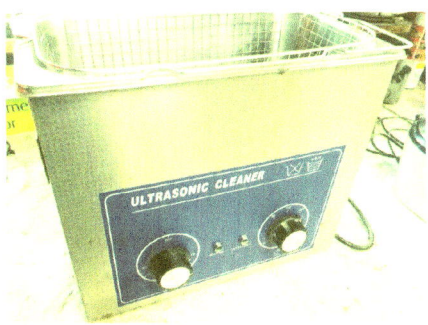

6.2 Smaller items such as carburettors can be thoroughly cleaned in an ultrasonic cleaner. These come in a variety of sizes. The smaller ones are suitable for cleaning very small parts such as carburettor jets, while the larger ones can take the entire carburettor. This is by far the best way of cleaning carburettors.

6.3 A carburettor before ultrasonic cleaning.

6.4 The same carburettor a few minutes later. Not only is the outside clean, but, more importantly, the tiny passageways inside the body are, too.

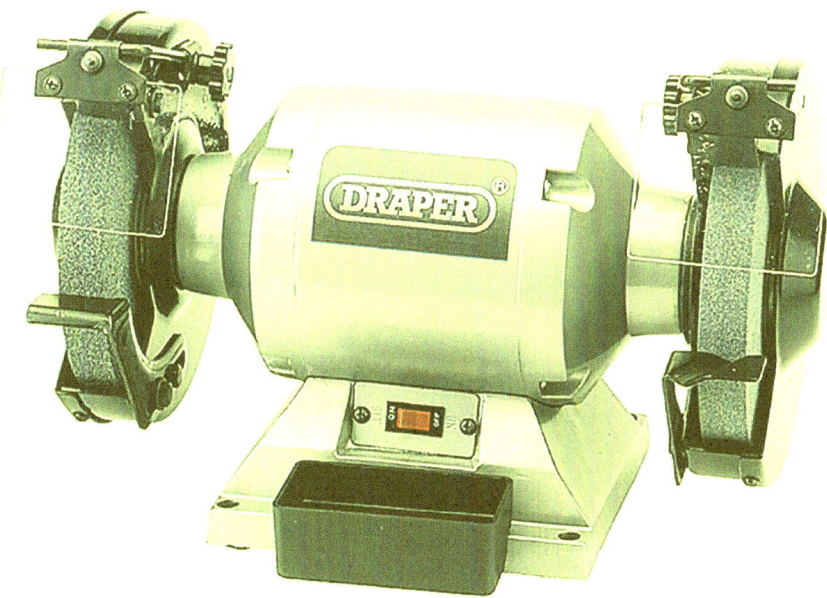

6.5 Polishing wheels have been adapted to fit a wide range of garage equipment, the most common of which is the bench grinder.

6.6 With the grinder bolted to your bench, you can apply the required pressure to the part being polished.

6.7 One of the grinding wheels removed and replaced by the polishing mop mandrel. The mandrel is a spiral attachment that allows quick and easy fitting and removal of polishing mop heads. You can also purchase dedicated polishing machines.

CLASSIC MOTORCYCLE RESTORATION

6.8 The polishing mop is screwed onto the mandrel, and the rotation of the spindle keeps the mop tightly fitted to the mandrel.

6.9 Attachments are also available for pillar drills and hand drills.

METAL POLISHING WHEELS AND COMPOUNDS

Alloy responds well to polishing, and with the correct equipment anyone can achieve great results.

Alloy parts, such as fork legs, engine casing, and control levers, can be polished to a high standard. Polishing kits are great value for money, and come with a selection of polishing wheels and compound bars of different grade polishing wax. The wax slowly melts away leaving the abrasive to polish/cut the metal. If too much wax is used, a residue will be left on the metal surface. This can be removed with white spirit and a clean cloth.

Polishing is much the same as sanding, using progressively finer and finer abrasives, each one cutting out the marks left by the previous one.

The combination of different grade polishing waxes and polishing mop wheels will leave a high-shine finish once the process is complete.

Polishing compounds

Brown – For first cut and flattening on nonferrous metals.
Blue – For final finishing on nonferrous metals.
Black – For first cut and flattening on steels.
Green – For final finishing on steels.
Pink – For final high polish finishing on chrome and steels.
White – For final high polish finishing on stainless steels.
Rouge - For polishing soft precious metals such as gold and silver.
Vienna Lime (White Powder) – For removing polishing compound and grease residues.

Polishing mops

There are three grades of polishing mops:
• Sisal metal polishing mops. These are very fast cutting and hard. They are used for first stage polishing operations, with brown metal polishing compound on soft metals, including aluminium, brass, and copper; and black metal polishing compound on hard metals, including steel and stainless steel.
• Colour stitch metal polishing mops. These are versatile cutting mops used for general metal polishing, which can be used for first stage polishing with brown metal polishing compound on soft metals, including aluminium, brass and copper; or for second stage polishing on hard metals with the green, pink and white metal polishing compounds.
• Loose fold metal polishing mops. The most popular, these mops can be used with the blue, green, pink, white and rouge metal polishing compounds. Loose fold metal polishing mops are 100% white soft cotton, with no hard pieces. The mops have centre washers, no staples, and are finished so they can be used straight away.

The polishing kits will not remove metal. If any of the parts are heavily scratched, marked, or scored, suitable abrasives should be used, such as a fine file, wet and dry paper, and rubbing blocks.

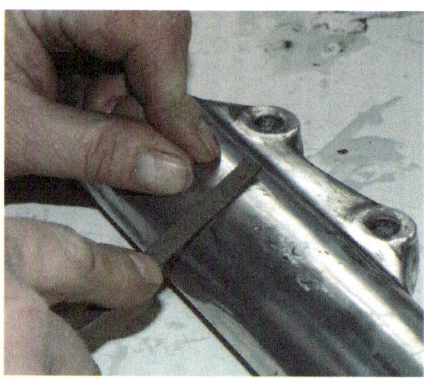

6.10 If you find that your alloy has some deep scratches, remove these before polishing. Use a fine metal file, and file lightly in different directions until the scratch or dent is gone.

6.11 Once the scratch is filed out, with some wet or dry paper of around 400 grade, sand the filed areas, making sure to dip it regularly in some clean water and soap solution. This removes the alloy particles, and keeps the paper clean and effective.

Once the marks left by the file have been sanded, change to 600 grade paper and continue sanding until the marks left by the 400 grade paper have been removed. Continue until you get a completely smooth surface ready to be polished. Cleaning and degreasing – with appropriate degreaser for the part – is essential prior to polishing.

Begin with the coarser, harder polishing wheel, known as sisal.

Once the drill or polisher is rotating, lightly touch the mop head with the grey wax bar, applying sparingly for two seconds. The dark grey bar is a coarser compound than the white bar, and should be used first.

CLEANING & POLISHING

6.12 Press the piece to be polished against the wheel, applying medium to hard pressure. Go over the entire surface several times until the worst oxidisation has been removed. Always try to vary the direction of the polishing mop over the surface, even if only by a few degrees. This may not always be possible, and will depend on the shape of the item you are polishing. If you come across scratches, try to polish across them rather than along.

When all scratches/marks are removed and the part has a uniform matt finish, remove the sisal metal polishing mop. It is very important that you remove all marks/scratches and leave a uniform finish for each grade of wax used.

Repolish with the softer wheel just like before, and go over the entire area of the piece you are polishing. Patience is the key here. If you require a very high polished finish, keep going over the piece with finer polishing bars until you reach the shine you are happy with. Using a clean cloth, go over the polished article with the white Vienna lime powder, which will remove any grease left on the surface. Then buff with a clean cotton cloth to finish.

Use smaller mops for difficult-to-reach areas.

Chrome polishing

Chrome-plated parts are always the focus of attention on motorcycles, and it's satisfying when your hard work begins to shine, literally. On smaller parts, use cream pastes like autosol or other chrome polishes with a clean cloth, to clean and remove light rust.

6.13 This is the finished fork leg, looking good as new. Polishing can be taken further if you require a mirror finish.

6.14 A selection of indicators in need of a good polish.

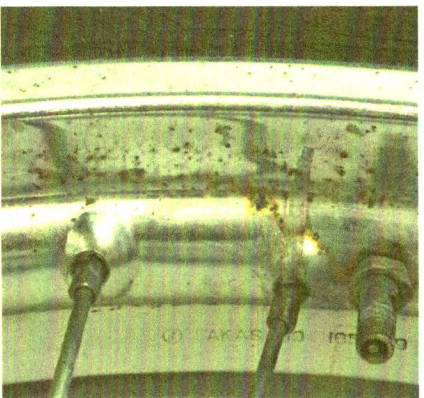

6.15 Light rust on this wheel rim can easily be removed with a suitable chrome polish.

On larger parts you can use the polishing wheels as you did with the alloy parts, but use the soft wheel and fine wax right away. There is no need to use wet or dry paper, or the coarser wax. These are too harsh for chrome.

6.16 Here is a good example of some serious polishing on a classic motorcycle. You wouldn't believe that this bike is almost 40 years old!

RUST REMOVAL

Many parts will inevitably have some degree of rusting. This could mean some parts are completely corroded and no longer of any use. Other parts may not be in such bad condition.

There are products on the market that will remove light surface rust, and, sometimes, help to loosen rusted parts, or even remove some quite bad rust completely.

On lightly rusted parts you can use any mild acid, such as vinegar or lemon juice, even cola. Soaking the required parts overnight is the easiest option – allow plenty of time to get good results.

On larger and more difficult parts, put the parts to be treated into a

CLASSIC MOTORCYCLE RESTORATION

large bowl. An old plastic baby bath is perfect because it is usually large enough to take most parts from a motorcycle. The parts will need to be degreased first – use a degreaser and a small brush to remove all grease and dirt, then rinse as instructed by the manufacturer.

Many rust removers are concentrated, and can be diluted to make around 20 litres of solution. Most need to be at room temperature to work effectively, and parts are usually left overnight to soak. Follow the instructions supplied with your particular rust remover. Once everything is cleaned, you can decide if any parts need to be sent off for re-plating.

After using any rust remover, rinse the cleaned part and administer a light spray of light oil, such as GT-85, to prevent rust returning.

For more heavy-duty rust or paint removal, you could use a shot blasting cabinet such as the one below. This works on compressed air from a compressor, and blasts different grades of media at high pressure onto the piece being cleaned, removing all rust back to the metal.

These are also used on engine crankcases, heads and barrels.

6.17 After the rust is removed, many parts – such as these Suzuki 'S' bolts – can be buffed on the polishing wheel and re-used.

6.19 A small cabinet blaster is an asset to your workshop. These connect to a compressor and have a blast gun inside the cabinet. Different grades of blast media are added to the cabinet and item can be placed inside to blast off rust and dirt. The media is recycled inside the cabinet and can be used several times. This is a dry process, and any item that needs to be blasted should first be free from grease.

6.18 The footrest on the right spent ten minutes in rust remover. This needed to be dried quickly to prevent rust forming again.

6.20 The exhaust port on a cylinder barrel, requiring cleaning before a rebuild.

CLEANING & POLISHING

6.21 The same cylinder barrel as in picture 6.20, after a few minutes in the blasting cabinet, with all carbon deposits now removed. This is a quick, clean process, and recommended for numerous motorcycle parts prior to refitting.

Before I purchased my first blast cabinet, I had enquired about having some parts cleaned. The price I was given for blasting two parts was over half the cost of the blasting cabinet, so the one I bought soon paid for itself. Although it is an effective tool for cleaning heavily soiled and rusted parts, you should proceed with caution with soft alloys and other delicate surfaces. These cabinets are powerful, and must use the correct blast media according to the surface being blasted. For a motorcycle sidestand made of steel, you could use a coarse media such as iron, whilst for a cylinder barrel – as in pictures 6.20 and 6.21 – you would use crushed walnut shells, which are much softer, and therefore don't damage the part.

DIY CHROME PLATING

Classic motorcycles have a large proportion of the visible metal chrome-plated. This gives a pleasing appearance, and protects the base metal underneath. A finished bike when polished is the pride and joy of the owner, who can spend hours polishing it. Unfortunately, over the years road grime and salt can take its toll on chrome plating, resulting in rust and pitting.

You have several options. You can polish these areas with some off-the-shelf chrome polish, or replace it with a good condition secondhand part.

You can also send your part to be re-chromed. There are many companies that offer this service, and the results can be very good, with the finished article looking like new. It is by far the best option, albeit not the cheapest.

Failing all the above, you could try DIY chrome plating. Kits have become more readily available over the last few years, and can give (with a little patience and practice) some acceptable results. Most DIY kits are more suited to the smaller parts of your bike. Brackets, nuts, bolts and spindles all add to the overall look of your bike. The dome bolts that hold down your handlebar clamps, the heads of the nuts and bolts that hold the front and rear mudguards (fenders) are in full view and always in chrome. These bolts could be replaced, however many manufacturers have their logo stamped on bolts – for example, Suzuki puts a small 'S' mark on many bolts – therefore check before replacing. Once stamped they will be difficult to source, so restoring them might be a better option.

Replica chrome plating kits give a good enough finish to satisfy the average restorer, can be quite easy to use, running off a simple small car battery charger, and are relatively inexpensive. They do not take up much room, and – you will like this – in the long run they will save you good money. There are some chemicals involved, but all kits come with instructions that include safety advice, which you should follow. The instructions can also often be found on the manufacturer's website, and it is worth reading these beforehand to help you decide whether this option is suitable for you.

The basic kit consists of:
Replica chrome electrolyte chemicals (will make five litres)
Replica chrome brightener
Replica chrome maintenance
Replica chrome anodes
A thermostatic tank heater
A tank
Titanium wire
Copper wire
Brown wire
Blue wire
A variable current controller, which enables you to use a 6-12v car battery or charger to plate various sized items
Crocodile clips
Goggles
A dust mask
Gloves
A replica chrome electroplating guide
Safety data sheets

Chapter 7
The engine

There is a wonderful array of motorcycle engine designs, and I admire all that I come across, as they all have plus and minus points.

Putting aside the amount of cylinders, motorcycle engines are generally split into two categories: 2-strokes and 4-strokes. There are also rotary engine motorcycles, but these are few and far between, and it's unlikely you'll come across one.

Japanese manufacturer Honda first began exporting motorcycles in the early 1950s, and was the largest motorcycle manufacturer in the world by 1959, maintaining its market share right up to the present day. Honda has developed, tested and used practically every engine design going, and is known to be at the forefront of motorcycle development. Honda has used a lot of its race technology in road-going motorcycles over the years.

7.1 A Honda CB750 single overhead cam 4-stroke, with four carburettors and a 4-into-4 exhaust system. Originally introduced in 1969, this is recognised as a milestone in motorcycle history, and often called the first super bike. Honda produced many four-cylinder, road-going motorcycles with essentially the same engine as here, ranging from the CB350F, CB400F, CB500F, CB550F, to the CB750, before moving onto double overhead cam engines, and then water cooling.

7.2 This is the Honda CBX 1000. The engine is a six-cylinder twin overhead cam air-cooled type. One of my favourite engines, with each cylinder having a separate carburettor and with a 6-into-2 exhaust system. Honda showing once again its engineering capabilities. In the 1960s Honda raced a six-cylinder 250cc motorcycle with great success.

THE ENGINE

7.3 Honda's biggest success, however, was in the small motorcycle market, and the single cylinder 4-stroke engine with one carburettor and a tiny exhaust seen in this little ST70 has been produced in various forms for over 50 years. Single cylinder engines are popular, and can be up to 600cc in capacity.

7.6 This is a Suzuki GT750 2-stroke triple, and the first Japanese motorcycle to have water cooling. It has a 3-into-4 exhaust system with a carburettor for each cylinder. There were two smaller versions – the GT380 and the GT550 – however, both of these were air-cooled.

7.7 This Yamaha XS650 is an example of an air-cooled twin-cylinder 4-stroke engine with two carburettors and a 2-into-2 exhaust system. This engine arrangement is very popular with all motorcycle manufacturers.

7.4 This is a four-cylinder air-cooled twin-cam engine with four carburettors running into a 4-into-4 exhaust system. This was a treat to find such a rare motorcycle. At first I thought it was just a Kawasaki Z900, which is rare enough to find in this condition. However, it turned out to be the 750cc version, which was only ever sold in the Japanese market.

7.8 This Yamaha RD350 is a great example of a 2-stroke twin engine with a carburettor and exhaust for each cylinder. This engine type was very popular because of its high power-to-weight ratio and low production costs. This design was used by many manufacturers.

7.5 Staying with Kawasakis, here is an H2 750cc 2-stroke triple with three carburettors using a 3-into-3 exhaust system. With around 75hp these were, let's say, interesting to ride, and needed to be treated with respect. Kawasaki made this in engine sizes ranging from 250cc to 750cc.

7.9 This is an interesting custom project, and clearly shows BMW's 4-stroke flat twin-cylinder 'boxer' engine with two carburettors and 2-into-2 exhaust system. These engines had a reputation for reliability, but with noisy gearboxes.

CLASSIC MOTORCYCLE RESTORATION

7.10 The wonderful engine layout of this Moto Guzzi Le Mans is a great example of a 4-stroke V twin engine with two carburettors running into a 2-into-2 exhaust system. This motorcycle also has shaft drive to the rear wheels in place of the most common chain drive. This example was spotted at a classic motorcycle race meeting.

ENGINE UNIT

In the second part of this chapter we look more closely at the engine unit, to give you a good basic knowledge of what you are likely to come across when stripping and rebuilding it, and what to look for while doing so.

This chapter is not a rebuild guide for your engine. There is a comprehensive range of motorcycle manuals that give very good step by step guides to stripping and rebuilding an engine, and, with the correct tools, many tasks are not difficult to achieve by the first time restorer.

Although some work may need to be carried out by a motorcycle engineer because of the precision required, there are some tasks you can perform yourself. You can save a huge amount of money if you do decide to rebuild, or at least carry out some repairs to the engine yourself. The feeling you get when you first start an engine that you have built and set up is great. Better still, if you have gone to the trouble of carrying out your own rebuild, and anything does go wrong at a later date, you're more likely to have the know-how to solve the problem.

With the engine safely on your bench and cleaned with a suitable degreaser, begin your inspection. Have a good look at it. Do you notice any cracks or leaks? Any screws or bolts with damaged threads? There are almost always some, and you have to get them out before proceeding with internal inspection.

WHAT YOU WILL NEED

There are certain parts on all engines that it is advisable to change during your restoration project. Some are service parts, and others mechanical.
1. A gasket set. Always buy a full engine gasket set, even if you do not always strip the entire engine. The spare gaskets and seals will come in useful later, and buying the bigger set is more cost effective than buying individual gaskets. Some seals are not included in some sets, so check first, and try to get hold of these separately if needed.
2. Fresh oil. Buy the oil recommended by the manufacturer. Don't forget a new oil filter, too, if your bike uses one.
3. Sparkplugs and air filter.
4. Clutch plates. These are consumable parts that wear during normal use. Clutch plates are not expensive, are easy to source, and not difficult to replace.

These are general procedures common to many engine types. Refer to the user manual for your specific motorbike when carrying out the following tasks.

WHAT TO LOOK FOR ON AN EXTERNAL INSPECTION

This can be done with the engine still in the frame.

7.11 Damaged fins. Generally, fin damage is only a cosmetic issue, and does not affect engine performance unless the fins are severely damage, which could lead to engine cooling problems. Damaged fins will certainly affect the resale value of your motorcycle.

7.12 Damaged threads and heads. It is likely that you will come across some damaged threads and bolt or screw heads on your project. These are repairable (see page 15). The main damaged thread to look for is the sparkplug thread. If this is very badly damaged it could mean a machine shop fix, and be a little expensive. However, it is repairable.

7.13 Kickstart and gearbox shafts. Check that these shafts have good splines – often they are badly worn. This will require a replacement, because it is not easy to repair properly, or while the shaft is still inside the engine.

7.14 Damaged casings or crankcase. Check for cracks and oil leaks, particularly in motorcycles that may have been used off-road and had a harder life. Small cracks can be repaired. However, this is not how a repair should look.

THE ENGINE

WHAT TO LOOK FOR ON A SEMI-INTERNAL INSPECTION

Remove side covers to assess parts of the engine, such as the clutch and starter mechanism. Ensure you drain the oil into an appropriate container before removing the engine side covers.

The colour of the oil will give you a good indication of the engine's internal condition. The oil should look like a rich honey and be clear – not milky white or black looking. It should be smooth to the touch, and not gritty.

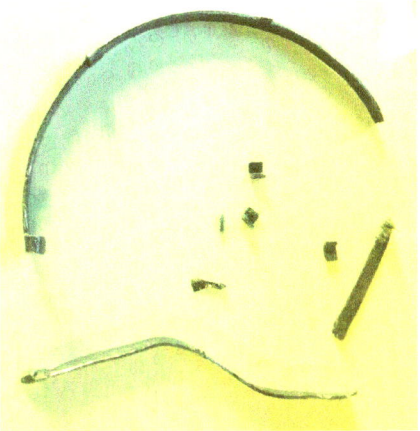

7.17 In water-cooled engines, if the oil looks milky, as left, water has penetrated into the engine, most likely via a bad head gasket or faulty seal. Determine which and rectify before putting the engine back together.

7.18 Broken clutch basket parts found after the side cover was removed.

7.15 With the clutch cover off, things look to be in a very bad way ...

7.19 Once the clutch cover is off, all parts should look reasonably clean, as seen here. There should be a visible film of oil over the engine parts, with all mechanical parts appearing sound. Look for broken metal pieces in the bottom, and visible breaks or damage. All nuts and bolts on the inside of an engine should be in very good condition; any damaged pieces should be replaced. If your clutch plates are worn or damaged replace them, too.

7.16 After removing the clutch basket, the clutch plates were found in pieces. Some smaller pieces were discovered in the bottom of the clutch housing.

49

CLASSIC MOTORCYCLE RESTORATION

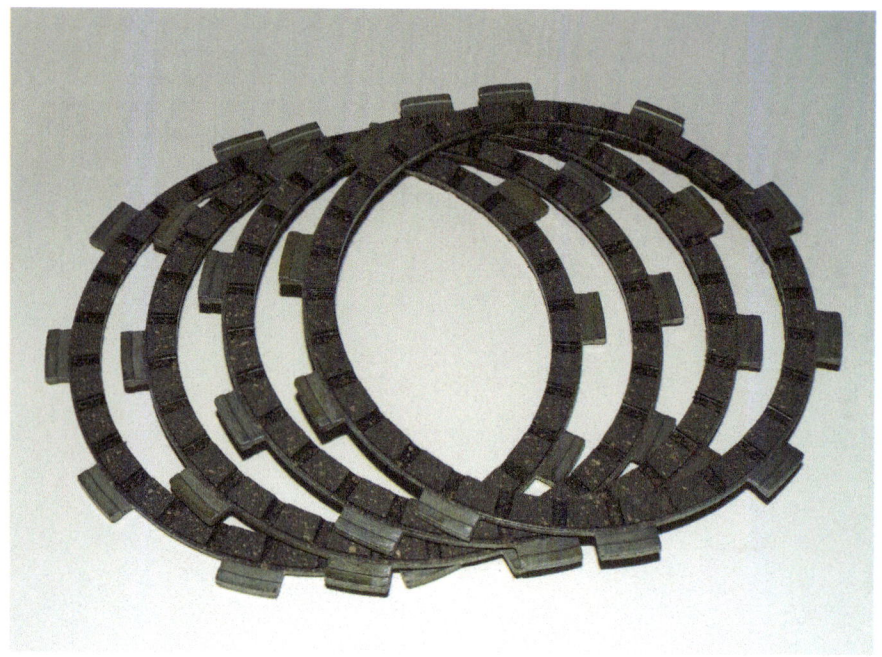

7.20 Replacing clutch plates is a very easy task, and with a new set being relatively inexpensive, I recommend always replacing old with new.

7.21 New clutch plates fitted to the clutch basket.

7.22 Next, you need to remove one of the casings that will allow access to the end of the crankshaft. (This is most likely the generator cover or the ignition cover.) Either will allow you to feel for end play (slack) in the crankshaft. There should be no sideways movement – if there is, it indicates worn bearings: a problem which must be corrected. This is not usually easy to rectify, and therefore should be carried out by a professional. I discuss this at the end of the chapter.

2-STROKE ENGINES

The 2-stroke, or 2-cycle engine as it is also known, is of a simpler design than the 4-stroke. It does not have cylinder head valves, cams, cam chains, tappets, or pushrods, so there is no valve adjustment or valve timing to carry out.

2-strokes engines revved much higher than the early 4-stroke engines, and, being lighter, they had a better power-to-weight ratio. The power delivery of a 2-stroke engine is usually more peaky then that of a 4-stroke, which usually has a lower rev range, but more low down engine torque. Motorcycles with 2-stroke engines are generally considered to be more 'thirsty' (use more fuel) than those with 4-strokes of a similar capacity.

All 2-stroke engines use a 2-stroke oil and petrol mix. On older motorcycles, the oil was mixed together with the petrol in a fuel can, then poured into the fuel tank premixed. Later manufacturers designed bikes with a separate oil tank and oil pump that mixed the oil automatically as you rode. Yamaha had the Autolube

THE ENGINE

7.23 A cutaway Yamaha twin-cylinder 2-stroke engine, showing the inlet port, piston, and exhaust port, along with the clutch mechanism.

This made the engines increasingly unpopular due to pollution and emission controls, and now, sadly there are no new bikes made with 2-stroke engines, other than very small capacity models. Generally, there is less maintenance to carry out on a 2-stroke engine.

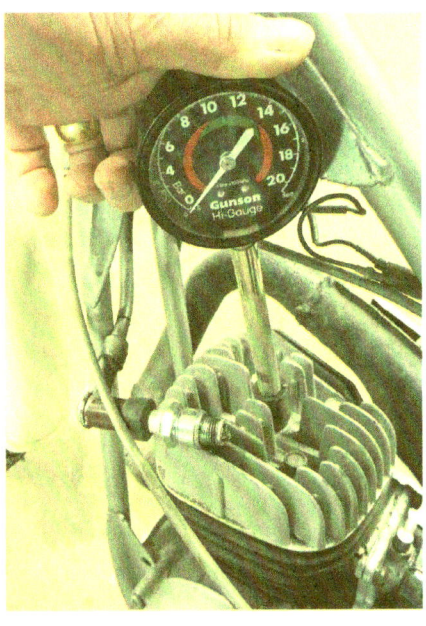

7.25 You can get a good indication of the cylinder condition by carrying out a compression test. This applies to 4-strokes as well as 2-strokes. Low compression level in a cylinder indicates a leak in the engine, most likely caused by worn piston rings or a damaged head or base gasket, requiring more investigation. Correct compression levels for your engine can be found in your workshop manual.

system, and Suzuki its CCI system. These systems seemed to use less oil, and were much more convenient for the rider. There was either an oil reservoir viewing window or a low oil warning light; sometimes both.

The biggest disadvantage of the 2-stroke engine was that it burned oil. To keep the engine lubricated, the oil had to be mixed with the petrol, meaning all 2-strokes emitted light blue smoke from the exhaust.

If the compression is too low, take a more thorough look by removing the cylinder head.

The cylinder head on a 2-stroke can be unbolted and taken off in a few minutes, and bolted back on with a new gasket. This gives you a good idea of the condition of the engine, and a look at the cylinder bores and piston crown, as well as the underside of the cylinder head itself. Remember that the head bolts should be unbolted in the order shown in your workshop manual, and tightened in the same order, and to a specific degree – this is called the torque. You need a torque wrench to do this. The torque settings are listed in your workshop manual.

7.24 A Suzuki side panel with the oil reservoir viewing window.

CLASSIC MOTORCYCLE RESTORATION

7.26 This is a 3-cylinder Suzuki GT750 2-stroke engine with head bolts removed. Note how thin the head is compared with a 4-stroke cylinder head, this is because there is no valve mechanism on a 2-stroke.

7.29 Before you remove the cylinder block, check whether any oil or water pipes are attached, and, if so, remove them.

Now is a good opportunity to de-coke the cylinder head. This is simply removing all old carbon deposits back to the metal. Try not to scratch the head while removing the carbon.

7.27 This is a 2-stroke head from a 3-cylinder Suzuki, after de-coking.

7.28 The cylinder bores after cylinder head removal. Note the water passages in this water-cooled cylinder block.

7.30 Once the cylinder block/barrels are fully removed, use some clean cloth to prevent debris falling into the crankcase. Now check the piston rings, and properly measure the piston itself. You can also see whether there is any play (movement up and down) in the big and small end bearings. There should be none. If there is, replace the bearings.

Do not let anything drop into the cylinder bores. Use some clean cloth to block the bore you are inspecting. If something drops into the cylinder, it will most likely find its way into the engine crankcase, which means a major engine stripdown.

Check whether the bores are scratched or scored. Check the gap between the piston and the cylinder. The tolerances will be in your workshop manual. The piston crown should be tan in colour. This gives an indication of how rich or lean the engine was running. Too dark and the engine is running too rich, too light and the engine is running too lean. A 2-stroke engine that is running too lean can seize, so it's really important to check this and set the fuel mixture correctly.

Once you have checked the bores and pistons, go to the next step and remove the cylinder barrels. If the bore on the cylinder was acceptable, there is no need to remove it, but if you do need to, you have to remove the carburettors and exhaust system first.

Slowly pull up the barrels. Sometimes they are willing, other times they need a little persuasion. If the barrel is stuck firm, give it a gentle tap all around with a rubber mallet to help free it. Usually this does the trick. Try to tap somewhere firm – not on any of the cooling fins if you can help it.

Once you have broken the seal and the cylinder begins to rise, as already mentioned, do not let anything drop into the crankcase. Use more clean cloth, and be careful. Continue to lift the barrel. You may have a single barrel or separate barrels. Remember the pistons will be at different heights if you have a multi-cylinder engine. You may need an assistant, because

THE ENGINE

you must lift the barrel whilst trying to hold the connecting rod (or conrod, as it is commonly known), which is now exposed. If you can hold the conrod, it will prevent the piston falling and hitting the barrel studs.

7.31 You may find that the piston rings are worn and need replacing. Note the small peg, and the shape of the ring ends that go under it, to ensure the piston rings are the correct way round.

7.33 Three new pistons and a new cylinder base gasket.

7.32 The crown of a piston. The arrow is to help you ensure the piston is facing the right direction. This piston needs to be de-coked.

If there are no scores in the cylinder or problems with the piston, count yourself lucky – it is unlikely you will need to carry out a rebore (if the compression was good, that is).

If you find you have a scored barrel or cracked piston, have the cylinder rebored and a new oversize piston fitted. The reboring should be carried out at a professional engine service workshop. It's usual when changing the piston to renew the small end bearing at the same time.

Don't forget to replace the cylinder base gasket before putting back on the barrel/cylinder block.

When you come to replace the piston and put back on the head, it helps if you have piston ring compressors to hold the rings in place when lowering the barrel. However, you can manage without these if you are careful, by simply squeezing the rings and holding them until the cylinder has slipped over. It does become a little tricky on a multi-cylinder engine, though.

Lightly oil the cylinder with a small amount of 2-stroke oil so the piston slips in nicely. It should go in reasonably easily – never force it. If it gets stuck, it is most likely that the barrel is caught on part of the piston ring. Ensure the rings are the correct way up, and that the piston and rings are facing in the right direction – usually there is a small peg in the piston ring groove, where the two ends of the piston ring should be to help ensure this. If the rings are over the pegs they will not sit back in the groove, and will catch on the piston.

Once the barrels are back on, replace the head gasket and the head. Now tighten the head bold/nuts in the right sequence, and to the torque described in your workshop manual. This is very important, and should be carried out correctly to ensure the head is not distorted and the gasket seats well.

You have now carried out a top end rebuild on your engine. Bottom end rebuilds are much more involved and most first-time restorers would leave a bottom end rebuild to the professionals. I will, however, go through the main procedures of a bottom end rebuild later in this chapter.

4-STROKE ENGINES

Many of the procedures in the 2-stroke section also apply to this section, and here I go through the main differences you come across when working on a 4-stroke or 4-cycle engine.

7.34 This is a small Honda 4-cylinder 4-stroke engine. Note the depth of the head due to the camshaft and valve gear when compared with the 2-stroke cylinder head (opposite page).

CLASSIC MOTORCYCLE RESTORATION

7.35 The cylinder head with rocker cover removed, showing camshaft, cam chain and valves.

scenario the piston could hit a valve, causing major engine damage.

Valves that are old may need to be changed, or at least re-lapped, which involves finely polishing the face of the valve and the valve seat, so the valve sits properly and gives a gas tight seal.

Certain components of the cylinder head need to be set precisely for the engine to run correctly. The camshaft needs to be set to match the crankshaft so that the cams are in the correct position for each valve relevant to each piston. The tappets need to be adjusted to the correct gap so that they open for the right amount of time.

If you want to inspect the piston on a 4-stroke, you have to reset all the above when you replace the head. Removing the head is more involved than if you were removing that of a 2-stroke, because you have the cam chain and camshaft to tackle. But, once the cam chain is loosened, you can pull out the cam and lift off the head.

The main difference between a 4-stroke and a 2-stroke engine is that the 4-stroke has inlet and exhaust valves that need a mechanism to drive them. The inlet valve opens to allow the fuel air mixture from the carburettor into the cylinder. It then closes, and both the inlet and exhaust valves stay closed for the compression stroke. The fuel air mixture is then compressed by the upward movement of the piston, and at the right time – usually a fraction before the piston reaches top dead centre – a spark is introduced by the ignition system, igniting the fuel and causing combustion.

Once the engine has fired the piston, it is forced down, and the exhaust valves open to allow the exhaust gas to escape. This happens thousands of times a minute, and has to be timed very precisely. Each valve has to open an exact amount – the tappets that operate the valves are usually adjusted by only a few thousandths of an inch. If the valves are adjusted incorrectly, they either open at the wrong time or for the incorrect amount of time, causing the engine to run badly or not at all.

The valves are operated by tappets that in turn are operated by either a pushrod, gears, or – now more

7.36 Here is a new, 50 oversize piston to match the rebored cylinder/s. Note the cutouts for the valves.

commonly – a camshaft or double camshafts. If they are operated by a camshaft, this will be run by a cam chain that has some sort of chain tensioner.

The bottom end of the engine has to be timed precisely with the top end, so that when the piston is at top dead centre (TDC) on the compression stroke, both valves are completely closed. If one is not properly closed there will be no compression, and the gas won't fire. In the worst case

7.37 Ensure you do not let the cam chain drop into the crankcase. Most workshop manuals advise tying a piece of wire or string to the cam chain in order to keep it raised, as seen in this photo.

If you have an older pushrod type engine, the head will come off more easily, but most classic Japanese 4-stroke bikes have overhead cam engines (OHC), or double overhead cam engines (DOHC).

If your 4-stroke engine has stood around for some time, it is likely that, when it starts for the first time (if you can get it to start before restoring it), it will smoke. Either the rings will be stuck in, allowing oil past, or the valve

THE ENGINE

stem seals will be ruined. Both of these will need to be rectified. On the whole, it is rare that you will get away with not rebuilding the cylinder head on a 4-stroke. You can attempt this yourself – there are some special tools needed such as a valve spring compressor – or you may conclude that, as with a bottom end build, this one is best left to the experts. If you decide to carry out this yourself, your workshop manual has a detailed step-by-step guide.

Inspecting the pistons, rings and ends is the same as with the 2-stroke engine.

THE BOTTOM END

I mentioned before that first time restorers are more likely to tackle a top end rebuild themselves, rather than a bottom end, which they are more likely to leave to the professionals.

Bottom end engine rebuilds are done in case of problems with a main bearing or a big end bearing. The main engine crankcases need to be taken apart to allow access to the crankshaft.

Then there is the crankshaft itself. This could well need a new main bearing, or need re-grinding. These procedures are carried out in an engine workshop by a professional.

7.39 This is quite involved, and means removing the clutch, the gears, the kickstart, and electric-start mechanism, along with other components ...

7.40 ... the process requires the use of at least a few special tools.

7.38 It may be the case that you have a damaged piston, and splitting the crankcase is necessary. You can see here parts from a broken piston skirt, which must be removed before rebuilding the engine.

7.41 This crankshaft seal was found to be split, so replacing it was unavoidable. The spring has broken out of its seal.

CLASSIC MOTORCYCLE RESTORATION

7.42 The crankshaft's component parts separated.

7.44 When the crankshaft is put back together, alignment must be checked thoroughly using dial gauges.

7.43 A heavy hydraulic press is needed to separate the crankshaft components: this is definitely a job for a professional.

Once the engine is fully stripped down you can replace all the seals and gaskets, inspecting parts such as the gears, clutch, etc as you go. Check with your workshop manual for all the parts to be replaced. If you are not so confident with an engine, you may want to let the professionals carry out bottom end work.

Chapter 8
Brakes, wheels & tyres

Almost every project I have been involved with has had brakes that needed restoring. In the past, I have bought projects that were seemingly almost finished, only to find on closer inspection that the front brake has only one bolt holding each calliper. Many advertised projects are loosely put together for photo shoots, and need thorough checking. So please take a very close look at all your brake system components.

I make it a rule now to refurbish all brake components as a matter of course on all my projects. Like carburettor rebuilds, it is not often you can get away with not doing it. This is one of my 'must do' tasks on every restoration project.

HYDRAULIC DISC BRAKES

First, check the brakes work and have no oil leaks. If they are free, not binding, and working okay, carry out checks to all the hoses and brake lines for splits and cracks, then check the brake pads or shoes for wear. If your project has been standing too long, the brakes will have very likely seized, and you need to rebuild them.

On first inspection, if you can get some movement from the brake pedal or lever, see whether you can free the brake calliper piston. This helps when rebuilding the calliper later, if required. Freeing the piston now, before you strip the system, saves hours spent trying to remove a seized piston later. The pressure from the master cylinder does all the hard work for you at this stage.

8.1 A dangerous brake hose with an obvious split. In all cases carefully check oil lines, rubbers, and seals for splits and leaks.

Most hydraulic systems that have not been used for a while suffer from non-uniform metal corrosion (the callipers are alloy and the piston is steel), and will be seized. It is also likely that the rubber hoses have perished and need changing.

The pistons in the master cylinder and the calliper corrode, and the rust makes them stick to the alloy body they are in. If the calliper pistons didn't move when you first tested them, they need to be freed before the brakes can work correctly.

Rebuilding the brake calliper

Here I use a Suzuki brake calliper as an example of what you are likely to find when restoring brakes. Please refer to the appropriate workshop manual for the correct method of rebuilding your callipers.

A seized piston can be freed in two ways. The first method, as mentioned, is to operate the brake master cylinder to push out the piston. However, this method will only work if your master cylinder is in good working condition. Often they are not.

8.2 A calliper in need of renovating. This must be stripped and rebuilt, including a fresh coat of paint.

CLASSIC MOTORCYCLE RESTORATION

8.3 The other way to free a piston is to remove the calliper from the bike. Block the brake hose hole with a suitably sized bolt, and attach a grease gun to the loosened bleed nipple. The pressure from the grease gun pushes out the piston. (This method has never failed me.) Once the piston is out, thoroughly clean and degrease the calliper.

8.5 A corroded piston. The chrome has come off in places, and if re-used would damage the rubber seal. The rust between the piston and the calliper bore made this piston seize in place.

8.6 The bare calliper – now is the best time to respray it (if it was painted originally). Depending on the condition of the paint, either give the entire calliper a good rub down with wet and dry abrasive paper until it is smooth, or, if the paint is very bad, use a paint stripper to remove it completely. If you do not have spraying equipment, a can of spray paint is fine. On such an exposed part of the bike I would use a harder-wearing paint such as Hammerite Smooth. Another advantage of using this type is that it is self-priming. If you choose to use cellulose paint, ensure the bare metal *is* primed first.

8.4 Now the piston is removed from the calliper, you will most likely find that the calliper bore is corroded, and needs thorough cleaning before you refit the new piston and seal. Use some wet and dry paper to remove the rust inside the calliper. It has to be completely clear of rust, and also very smooth to take a new rubber seal.

8.7 The black rubber seal here needs replacing. It can be prised out with a small screwdriver or similar.

BRAKES, WHEELS & TYRES

8.8 This calliper was cleaned in the blast cabinet and finally polished with 1200 grade wet and dry paper. It's now ready for the new piston and seal. Once you have resprayed the calliper body, fit the new seal.

8.11 Slide the new piston into the calliper. Applying a little brake fluid to the seal will help the piston slide in more easily.

8.9 New piston and dust cover. The seal is already fitted in the calliper.

8.12 On this calliper type there is a metal ring that holds in place the piston boot. These are often in very poor condition, and can break when you try to remove them. Gently prise off the ring evenly around the edge – you may be lucky and remove it in one piece.

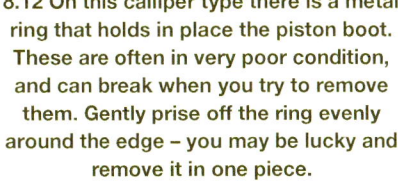

8.10 A cautionary note – in the photo above are two seals, both described and sold as suitable for a Suzuki GT750. The one on the left is an aftermarket part, and the one on the right is the original Suzuki part. With the seal on the left fitted, the brake calliper would not fit over the brake disc. The rubber is simply too thick. Using the original Suzuki rubber, the calliper fitted without problem. Although some aftermarket parts are okay, it is always better to fit originals, if available.

8.13 An aftermarket stainless steel ring was available for this calliper. This will last a lifetime, and was certainly worth the modest extra cost.

CLASSIC MOTORCYCLE RESTORATION

8.14 The ring fits inside the rubber boot, ready to be fitted to the calliper.

8.17 I always fit a new brake bleed nipple. Often the original will break off while you are trying to remove it.

8.19 The brake discs need to be checked for cracks. Although I have never come across a disc that wasn't re-useable on a motorcycle, they can be scored and may need machining or in extreme cases renewing. This is not the norm and most are thankfully in useable condition.

8.15 The ring with the rubber boot now fitted is flipped over and pressed into the calliper body, around the new piston.

8.18 Calliper rebuilt, complete with new bleed valve. Two or three coats of paint makes the calliper look like new.

it is unlikely your master cylinder is seized, but it is still worth considering rebuilding if it did not push fluid through enough to move the calliper piston. Give everything a good external clean.

Carefully begin stripping the master cylinder. The procedure is slightly different depending on the bike model so refer to your workshop manual before carrying out the correct procedure.

This is the most common procedure.

8.16 Always fit new crush washers to the brake hose banjo bolt. These come in either copper or aluminium.

When the paint has dried and the calliper is cleaned and polished, it is ready for the new piston and seal kit. Rebuild the calliper in the reverse order of stripping down with the new seals and disc pads, and put away until you are ready to refit them to your bike later. When you come to fitting the calliper back to your bike, bleed the system as described in your workshop manual. You can buy stainless steel calliper pistons for most bikes, and this is worth considering because these tend not to seize. If this option is too expensive, apply some copper grease to the piston below the seal line to prevent it seizing again.

REBUILDING THE MASTER CYLINDER

If your master cylinder is also seized, rebuild it. Rebuild kits are available for most motorcycles. Pull in the brake lever to see if there is any movement. If you can move the brake lever then

8.20 Begin by emptying all fluid from the reservoir into a suitable container, and discard in the correct manner. Remove the master cylinder from the handlebars by unscrewing the two bolts. Protect the paintwork from any brake fluid splashes as this will damage paint and decals.

BRAKES, WHEELS & TYRES

8.21 The brake pipes are likely to need renewing. If in a good condition, store them safely. Unscrew the brake hose banjo bolt. A small amount of brake fluid will leak out when you undo the bolt so have a cloth ready. If your paintwork is in good condition ensure no brake fluid comes into contact with it: brake fluid also acts as good paint stripper!

8.24 This master cylinder has been cleaned with the two holes showing and is now ready for rebuilding.

8.22 Once on the bench remove the brake lever by undoing the small nut and bolt. Note here that the hose bolt has been refitted for safe keeping.

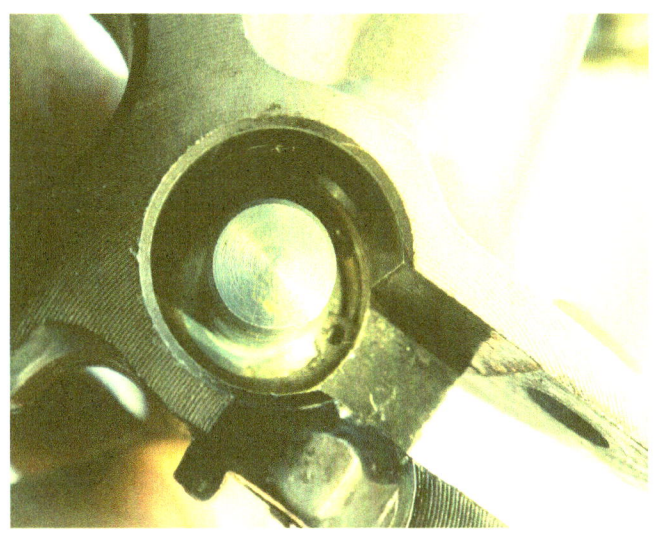

8.25 Inside, where the brake lever pushes onto the piston, there is a spring clip holding down the dust boot. Remove the spring clip then pull out the rubber dust cover. The dust cover on this master cylinder was already missing. Underneath is a circlip.

8.23 Remove the reservoir cap. Check inside and wipe as much as you can with a cloth to see if you can find the holes at the bottom of the reservoir. The inside of the reservoir is usually dirty and the two holes blocked. These too should be cleaned thoroughly, as they need to be free from debris to allow fluid to pass through.

CLASSIC MOTORCYCLE RESTORATION

8.26 Using long nose circlip pliers, remove the circlip. This can be a little awkward. I have found that sometimes the points of the circlip pliers are too large to fit into the circlip holes. In this case, grind or file the points to make them slimmer.

8.27 Now the piston can be pulled from the master cylinder. The cylinder will require cleaning and de-greasing ready for the new piston kit.

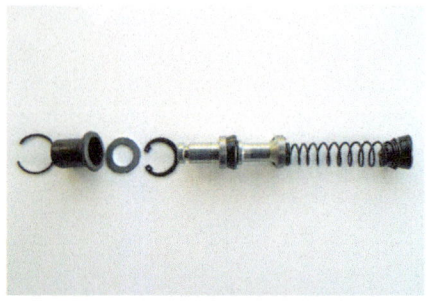

8.28 The new master cylinder piston and seal assembly ready to be fitted.

8.29 Now completely clean and degreased, fit the piston and seal kit.

Once this has been cleaned properly, fit the new piston and seal kit. Insert the new piston with seals into the master cylinder, and sit the new circlip on top of the piston. With your circlip pliers, squeeze the circlip just enough for it to slip into the master cylinder bore, and then release so that it sits inside the circlip groove. It is important to check that the circlip has actually gone into the slot. If it hasn't, the piston will pop back out.

Fit a new dust cover and spring clip to hold it in. The master cylinder is now rebuilt.

CABLE OR ROD DRUM BRAKES

Cable and rod-operated drum brakes are less of a problem to restore than hydraulic disc brakes, and mostly they only need stripping, cleaning, and reassembling with new brake shoes fitted.

Check all brake cables for the correct routing. A cable may have been put on quickly for the purpose of a photo, or to make the bike look more complete. A cable that is not routed correctly could tighten when the handlebars are turned, activating the brakes and catching you out when riding. This has happened to me in the past.

Check for frayed cables. They do not return correctly, and could result in sticky brakes, which bind and wear out prematurely.

Oiling cables

This method has been used for years, and is still effective today. It can be used on all cables on your bike.

Find somewhere that you can hang your cables quite high, so they don't touch the floor. Use a piece of plasticine to make a small funnel tight to the cable. Hang the cable and pour a small amount of light oil into the funnel. Ensure the cable is hung over a suitable container so that, if the oil eventually makes its way through, it will drip into the container. After 24 hours, try pulling the cable – it should move within its casing. If it is stuck firm, it is recommended you buy a new one.

BRAKES, WHEELS & TYRES

8.30 You can use plasticine to make a funnel around a cable and apply light oil to it. Overnight the oil will make its way down the entire length. This method will work on lightly corroded examples. I have in the past had cables that are so corroded they just snapped under light pressure. If you have any doubt about yours, change them. You don't want to be miles from home when a cable breaks. At best it is inconvenient; at worst it can be very dangerous.

WHEELS

On classic bikes, wheel rims come in plain steel, chrome-plated, stainless, and alloy, including spokes, and can be polished, painted, or powder-coated.

Often wheels are in poor condition, and you should check that the wheels are not buckled or damaged in any way. Check all the spokes for tightness. If you have alloy wheels, check for hairline cracks and chips in the alloy.

If you are lucky, a good clean and polish will bring your wheels up like new. If you are unlucky they may need rebuilding.

It can sometimes be cheaper to look around for a good used wheel, rather than have one completely rebuilt.

If the chrome plating on your wheels is in very bad condition, or the wheels are damaged, new rims can be bought. The wheels must be stripped down and completely rebuilt, with the spokes taken out and the hubs checked over before reassembly. Wheel rebuilding is a specialist job, and I would not advise an amateur to undertake this task.

However, there are other tasks that you can undertake that improve the overall appearance of your wheels. The brake discs often have a painted centre, which can be repainted, making a whole lot of difference to the finished look of your motorcycle.

Begin by removing the spindle and taking off the wheel. Remove the discs, tapping back the locking tabs so you can undo the bolts.

8.31 Almost all of the black paint on the brake disc centre has worn away here. You can also see how to tap back the locking tabs to enable you to undo the disc-retaining bolts.

Once you have removed all the retaining bolts, pull the disc away from the wheel.

Degrease the disc and dry it thoroughly. Tape off areas that are not going to be painted. Some difficult to tape areas could be sprayed, but make sure you remove the paint later on.

8.32 The main disc, taped and first coat applied.

The overspray in the centre will be covered by the disc itself, so will not need to be stripped off.

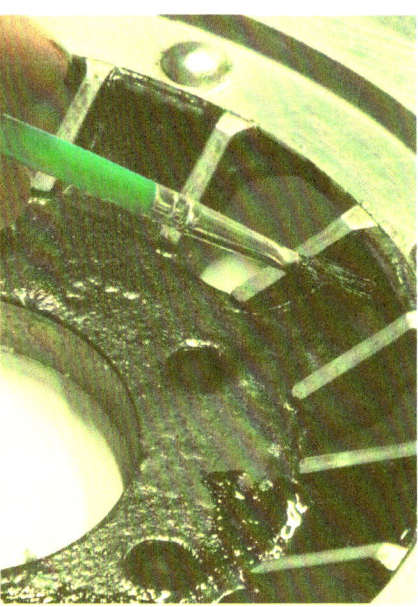

8.33 Use a small paintbrush for the difficult-to-reach areas.

8.34 The wheel with discs removed. Now is the time to polish the hub.

The hubs can be difficult to polish properly – use a small multitool with a polishing head to get into the hard-to-reach areas.

8.35 This rear brake hub hasn't seen polish for years.

63

CLASSIC MOTORCYCLE RESTORATION

8.36 Polishing the difficult areas with a multitool.

8.37 After a short time you will have a nicely polished hub.

TYRES

Tyre condition is an essential part of the road worthiness assessment of a bike. Any perishing, low tread, splits and cuts affect safety, and therefore it is well advised that the tyre be changed.

I have never had a restoration project where the tyres were in good enough condition to re-use. Always budget for a new set on your project, and don't forget to include the inner tubes and rim tape, too. Never mix worn with unworn tyres. All new tyres have a mark on them indicating their position: 'front' or 'rear.' It may sound obvious, but sometimes might be overlooked.

8.38 A tyre clearly marked for front use only. Arrow shows rotation direction.

Tyres should be changed in pairs, and be from the same manufacturer. They are designed to work together to keep optimum handling performance. The motorcycle manufacturer will have a recommended tyre, and there is likely to be a modern day equivalent if the original is no longer available.

Always fit new inner tubes when fitting new tyres. An old inner tube will be stretched, and can crease and fail due to the thin rubber.

8.39 A tyre showing clear signs of perishing. Both dangerous and illegal, if your tyre is worn or looks like this, renewal is the only option.

BRAKES, WHEELS & TYRES

Many tyre manufacturers still make tyres for classic motorcycles, which retain the classic look. However, many riders fit more modern tyres because they often give better grip and a more confident riding experience than the older type of tyre.

It is possible to change or fit tyres yourself using tyre levers, but if your project has been unused for some time you will find that the rubber has gone very hard, and will be almost impossible to change yourself. If you take your wheels to the motorcycle shop where you are buying tyres, the staff will fit the tyres for free. This is the best option, with the added benefit that the wheels are balanced at the same time – something you can't do at home.

Once the old tyre is removed, it is very likely that the inside of the rim, (under the inner tube) will have some areas of rust. The tyre fitter uses a wire brush to remove these, then fits rim tape, which is used to cover the heads of the spokes, so should any rust reappear it will not cause a puncture.

Here the fitter is about to fit the new Bridgestone tyre to the wheel. With the wheel tightly clamped to the machine, this job is much easier.

Be sure to ensure the correct tyre pressure for your motorcycle. Checking tyre pressure is the most important tyre maintenance function you can perform, and improves your safety on the road. Under-inflated tyres can result in imprecise cornering, higher running temperatures and overheating, irregular tread wear at the edge of the contact patch, and eventual failure.

8.41 Wheels tightly clamped and new rim tape fitted. The tape prevents the spoke heads from touching the inner tube.

8.40 After 20 years on the wheel, removing this tyre was a two-man job.

CLASSIC MOTORCYCLE RESTORATION

8.42 Ensure the fitter knows the direction of rotation of the wheel. It is not always obvious, and must be pointed out before the new tyre is fitted.

Over-inflating tyres will not increase load-carrying capacity, but it will result in a hard ride and accelerated tyre wear in the centre of the contact patch.

Check cold tyre pressure frequently with a good quality gauge that holds a reading, especially before long-distance trips.

8.44 Time to go now; other customers are waiting.

8.43 Lastly, the essential tyre pressure check. It is important to use the correct tyre pressure, otherwise safety and early wear problems can result.

8.45 The finished wheel and tyre combination, cleaned, repainted, and with new rubber. The tyres need approximately 100km or 60 miles scrubbing in before reaching optimum performance.

www.velocebooks.com
New book news • Special offers • Newsletter • Details of all Veloce books • Gift Vouchers

Chapter 9
Fuel system & exhaust

Whilst stripping the components, we had a quick look to assess the fuel system. Now it is time take a closer look. Any blockages in either the exhaust or fuel system results in poor running or not running at all.

THE FUEL TANK

It is paramount to ensure that any rust or scale is removed completely from the fuel tank. Even small particles will cause running problems by blocking the filters in the fuel tap or carburettor.

Rust remover can be used effectively on the inside of the fuel tank, followed by a resin fuel tank liner if necessary.

If the tank is more seriously contaminated it will need further cleaning. Begin by removing the fuel tap and setting aside for closer inspection later.

There are various methods of cleaning the inside of your tank. If it contains sludge and scale, one method is to place a few handfuls of small gravel (such as that found in the local pet shop for aquariums) in the tank and shake. This helps to abrade the inside and loosen the encrusted debris.

Find a way to block the fuel tap hole – a piece of cork from a wine bottle does the job. You do not want the rust removing fluid to leak out. Next, rinse the tank with a warm, soapy water solution. Empty out the water and dry the tank, then add the rust remover solution.

9.1 If the inside of your tank looks like this, it needs attention before you can put fuel in it. Fuel tanks often have rust, scale, or even old fuel that has turned to sludge at the bottom. Thoroughly clean this out before refuelling.

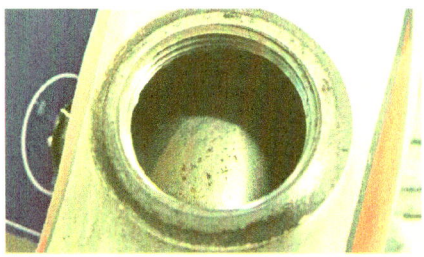

9.2 This tank shows only slight rusting and requires just a light clean. Rinse out the tank with a small amount of 2-stroke oil petrol mix. Swill around so the fuel reaches all corners of the tank, then empty into a suitable container. This clears out any particles, and helps prevent further rust.

If your tank was in particularly bad condition, you may want to consider lining it with a resin-based tank sealer. These also bind any rust scales that could not be removed, and fill any tiny pin holes.

Finally, carry out any cosmetic work to your tank. For further details, refer to the chapter on spraying.

If your tank wasn't in bad condition, add (once the fuel tap is refitted) some petrol mixed with a small amount of 2-stroke oil. Give it a light swill around to coat the sides of the

CLASSIC MOTORCYCLE RESTORATION

9.3 When the rust-removing process is complete, dry the tank thoroughly. I place mine on a small oil filled radiator at a low heat setting for a few hours. CAUTION! The tank may contain combustible fuel fumes. Whichever method you use, the tank needs to be completely dry to avoid rust build-up in the future.

tank and prevent rust reforming. You can use this method even if the bike is a 4-stroke.

Now set the tank aside until later.

FUEL TAP

Dismantle the fuel tap, being careful not to lose any small parts such as springs, screws etc.

When dismantling the fuel tap or carburettor, try to avoid tearing the gaskets or seals. Although it's recommended that you replace all of them, you may find it difficult to source some, and therefore may have to re-use one or two.

The fuel taps and carburettors can often be seized solid, requiring some gentle persuasion to release them. Soak them in light oil for a while to penetrate the threads and joints before attempting to remove them.

9.4 Unscrew the fuel tap from the tank, and put away the screws safely for use later. If there are any washers, these will usually need replacing. You will find at least one O ring or other rubber seal between the fuel tap and the tank. This is also likely to need replacing.

9.5 Once the fuel tap is off, place it on a clean surface ready for dismantling. A small amount of fuel is likely to spill when you remove the bowl, so it is a good idea to have some cloth ready.

9.6 Unscrew the fuel tap bowl. Be prepared for some fuel to spill.

9.7 It is usual to find some particles in the bowl. Note the condition of the rubber seal – save it if not damaged.

9.8 Once the bowl is removed you will see the fuel tap filter. Remove gently, clean with carburettor cleaner, and blow through with an airline.

9.9 and 9.10 Next remove the tap lever by unscrewing the faceplate screws. This is the most common way to remove the tap lever, but, as with the small Yamaha tap pictured, sometimes the lever is held in place by a single screw on the side of the tap body.

FUEL SYSTEM & EXHAUST

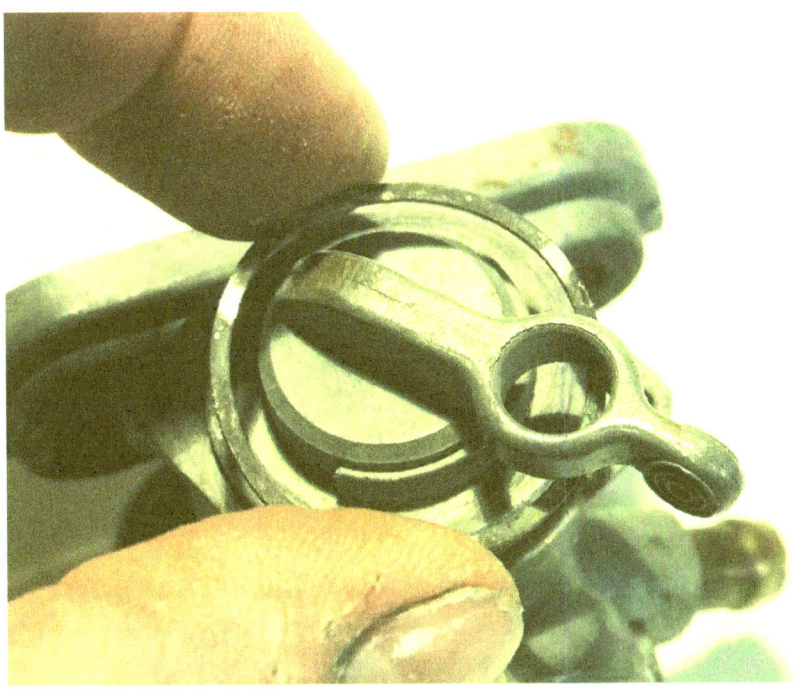

9.11 Once the faceplate is removed, there will often be a light spring that keeps the tap arm firm when in use.

9.14 Now you have only the fuel tap body remaining. At this stage you will be able to see the passages the fuel flows through. Every passage should be cleaned thoroughly. Use an airline to blow through them. If they are completely blocked, use a small pointed object – such as a watchmaker's-type screwdriver – to gently dig out the scale and clear the passages. Use carburettor cleaner when they are virtually clear to remove any varnish-like deposits.

9.12 and 9.13 Here, you can see the rubber seal. Gently lift this out using a small screwdriver. Try not to split the seal – it may be useful later.

9.15 and 9.16 Ideally, this is where you would use an ultrasonic cleaner. Small ultrasonic cleaners are inexpensive, and suitable for smaller items. When cleaning larger items such as the carburettor body, use the larger model. If you do not have one, use carburettor cleaner and a small pointed object to clear passages.

CLASSIC MOTORCYCLE RESTORATION

If the seals and gaskets came out in one piece it may be possible to re-use them, but it is always best to fit a rebuild kit if you can find one.

9.17 When everything is clean, rebuild the fuel tap in reverse order. Once fitted, it should work like new again.

9.18 Whether you have a multi-cylinder or single-cylinder motorcycle, begin by removing the air filter. Disconnect all cables and fuel pipes, leaving only the carburettors and rubbers to be removed.

THE CARBURETTOR

This section shows the stripdown and rebuild of a carburettor from a small single-cylinder Yamaha. The components are similar to most other carburettors, with only minor differences between makes and models. The workshop manual provides more details on your specific carburettor.

When dismantling, it is a good idea to take photos and notes so you know where the parts go when rebuilding.

The main objective of cleaning carburettors is to ensure all air and fuel passages are completely clean and free from obstructions, as they tend to get clogged whilst in use. On all projects I would recommend a full stripdown and rebuild of the carburettors, unless your bike was running flawlessly when you bought it.

The carburettor is connected to the cylinder in various ways. Some connections are rubber, some are a rubber/alloy combination, and others are alloy only. If you have a rubber connection, check for splits or perishing. If the rubbers are damaged, they need to be replaced.

9.19 Here, Suzuki has used a rubber-only connection between carburettor and cylinder.

The rubbers often go very hard over the years, becoming more like plastic. Loosen the clamps holding the rubbers and prise away. Next, see if you can pull the carburettors off the engine block.

9.20 On some Honda Fours, alloy/rubber combinations are used. Be very careful when trying to remove carburettors from a motorcycle that has not been used for years – the rubber can break away from the alloy, making the small manifold unusable. This type also uses a rubber O ring seal, which must be replaced with a new one.

FUEL SYSTEM & EXHAUST

9.21 This small carburettor is connected to the cylinder with an all-alloy reed valve block.

9.25 Simply unscrew the bolt and twist free the carburettor.

9.27 If you do not have a drain screw on your carburettor bowl, place the overflow pipes in a suitable jar and tip the carburettor until fuel runs out.

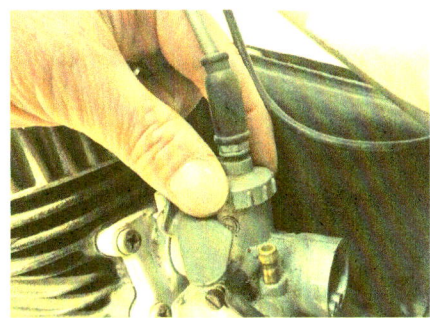

9.22, 9.23 Before removing the carburettor from the cylinder, pull out the carburettor slide. Unscrew the knurled top and lift out the slide.

9.26 Drain any fuel left in the carburettor bowl. On most carburettors there is a brass drain screw or bolt at the bottom of the bowl. Unscrew this over a container to catch the fuel.

Once removed, you need a very clean work area to begin dismantling your carburettors.

TIP! Find a small clean plastic container (eg margarine tub) for each carburettor. When dismantling, put all the pieces in the containers, keeping each carb's parts separate.

Clean the main body of the carbs to remove any dirt and grime before dismantling – this will help keep the inside clean afterwards. Dismantle one carburettor at a time.

9.24 Note the slot in the carburettor slide. This locates on a peg inside the carburettor body, to ensure the slide is fitted facing in the right direction.

9.28 Remove the bowl of the carburettor by unscrewing the four screws and set aside; try not to damage the bowl gasket. The fuel will run out, so have a container ready. Remember, **NO NAKED FLAMES!**

71

CLASSIC MOTORCYCLE RESTORATION

9.29 Once the bowl is off, take a look inside. This one is surprisingly clean.

9.32 The pin should push out quite easily, but if it doesn't, tap the object you're using with a hammer.

9.33 Once the float is removed, check it for pin holes. Put it in a bowl of warm water – if any bubbles appear, it means there are holes and the float needs to be replaced. If you have a brass float with holes, these can be repaired with a small spot of solder.

9.35 The jets are removed by using a small spanner and screwdriver. Replace the fibre washer if it looks damaged.

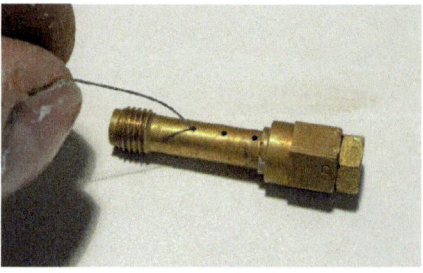

9.30, 9.31 The float is now visible, and can be removed by pushing out the metal pin using a small pointed object.

9.34 Inside the carburettor we can see the needle jet, main jet, pilot jet, float needle, and a seal.

9.36 Any particles that are firmly stuck will need to be pushed out with a piece of wire. Also flush with carburettor cleaner to remove any fine deposits.

FUEL SYSTEM & EXHAUST

9.39 Now, with only the main body remaining, thoroughly clean the inside and outside before rebuilding the carburettor. Rebuild in the reverse order of dismantling, using all clean or new parts.

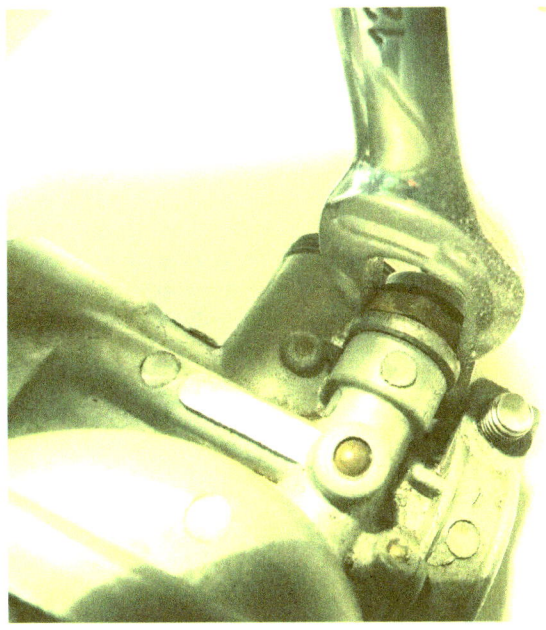

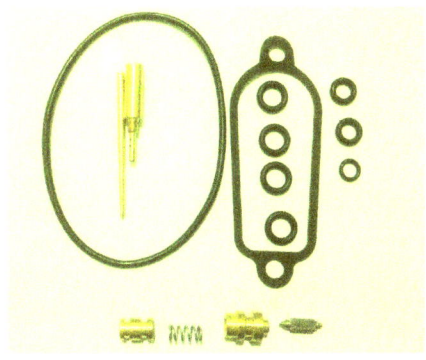

9.40 I would recommend that a carburettor rebuild kit be fitted – a genuine one if possible, but aftermarket kits are usually okay. This is a rebuild kit from a 1976 Honda CB400 Four Super Sport.

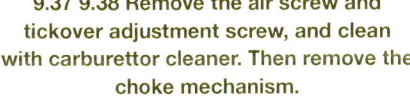

9.37 9.38 Remove the air screw and tickover adjustment screw, and clean with carburettor cleaner. Then remove the choke mechanism.

Before removing the air screw, screw it in fully with a screwdriver, noting the number of turns needed. When replacing the air screw, screw in fully and screw out the same number of turns noted before. This will help to get a basic fuel air mixture setting when rebuilding the carburettor.

9.41 This is a set of carburettors from a 1976 Suzuki GT750, with new fuel and overflow pipes fitted and an inline fuel filter, too.

CLASSIC MOTORCYCLE RESTORATION

Once the carbs are rebuilt, set the float height and jets according to your workshop manual. Now put the carbs in a clean container out of the way so no dust can contaminate them, ready to be put back on your engine.

THE EXHAUST SYSTEM

The exhaust system is often in poor condition with rusty holes and dented or scratched chrome. It is also one of the most difficult secondhand parts to find in good condition. New, original parts are not easy to find, and could be very expensive. Some aftermarket replicas are very good, but can be pricey, too. If you do not necessarily want your bike to be 100% original, there are many options open to you with off-the-shelf generic silencers easy to find. If you do buy an aftermarket exhaust, be sure it is for road use. Many exhausts are for race track use only, and are not legal on public roads.

9.44 This pair of new silencers was obtained at a motorcycle auto jumble swap meeting for a very reasonable price, and would make an excellent replacement to a twin with damaged original silencers. Very little maintenance is needed on the exhaust system, other than keeping it clean and clear of carbon deposits. On 4-strokes this is less of a problem, but on 2-strokes carbon can quickly build up from 2-stroke oil smoke.

9.47 and 9.48 Remove the screw or bolt, and pull out the baffle with a suitable pair of pliers. Baffles are quite long. Pulling while twisting the baffle from side to side will help to release it, and loosen the carbon holding it.

9.42 The acids in the exhaust fumes have caused this silencer to develop a hole. It will need a braze repair if a replacement is not available.

9.45 Check the baffles in the end of the exhaust system. Remove and clean according to your workshop manual.

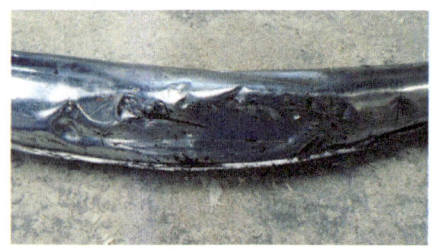

9.43 Damage caused by over-enthusiastic cornering or an accident is often seen on the exhaust system. This is not repairable, and needs replacing. If the damage is on the far underside of the exhaust and has not caused a split or a hole, you could consider re-using it, as it will not affect performance or safety.

9.46 There is a small hole on the underside of the exhaust. Inside the hole is either a screw or a bolt holding the baffle in place. Once this is removed, the baffles can be pulled out.

9.49 Once the baffles are out, use a small wire brush and some degreaser to remove the carbon. The heat-resistant wadding is missing from this baffle, and should be replaced.

FUEL SYSTEM & EXHAUST

9.50 Sheets of baffle wadding are inexpensive, and, with a pair of scissors, easy to cut to size.

9.51 Use a pair of wire cutters and some wire.

9.53 Roll the wadding tightly around the baffle.

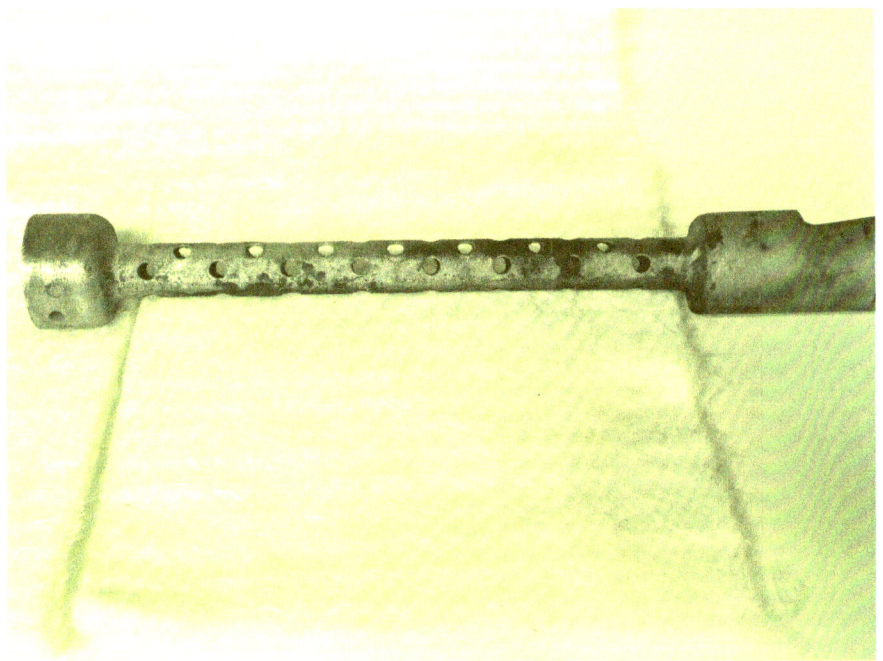

9.52 These baffles have been cleaned, with all the holes now visible. Place on the wadding to measure the correct size.

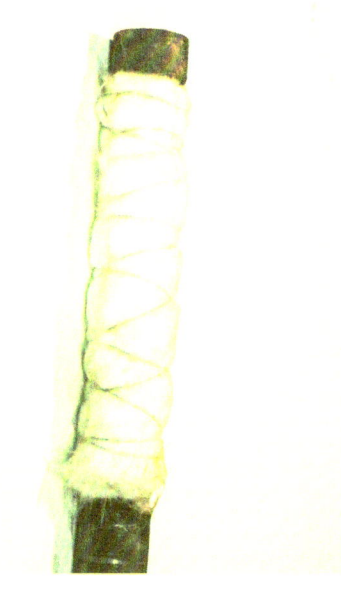

9.54 Secure tightly with the wire. Use the scissors to trim any excess wadding. The baffle is now ready to be refitted to the exhaust.

CLASSIC MOTORCYCLE RESTORATION

Check for cracks and holes in the exhaust system, which are likely to result in failure in a roadworthiness test. Check all joints for exhaust gas leaks. Gaskets and exhaust seals are usually available for joints and connecting to the cylinder head. Where possible, renew any seals between joints.

9.55 The exhaust pipe seal in the cylinder head is usually a large crush type washer that should be replaced whenever the exhaust has been removed. These are made of copper or aluminium.

9.56 With the original exhaust system hard to find in good condition, you may need to look for an alternative. These exhaust silencers are not original Honda – in fact, they are from a 500 Benelli – but nevertheless, they look great on this Honda, and still retain the 4-in-4 style originally found on the motorcycle.

Chapter 10
Electrics

Correctly operating electrics spare you future problems with engine starting and running, faulty lights, or, in the worst case scenario, fire. If the electrics are too damaged, starting afresh is the easiest and most recommended option.

Most electrical problems are solved simply by replacing the faulty part. Sparkplugs, points, and starter solenoids are all low cost parts that are not serviceable. The parts that are serviceable are more likely to be bigger items, such as the starter motor, the price of which is much higher, making it more suitable for repair.

FAULTS AND PRECAUTIONS
When taking electrical parts off your bike, be very careful with the connectors, and as mentioned before, always pull the connectors, not the wires. This way the wires will not come apart.

There are three reasons that electrics fail:

1. Open circuit faults: a wire that is broken or detached, causing a break in the electrical circuit

2. Short circuit faults: cuts in the wire, causing the wire to touch part of the frame, or other adjacent part.

3. Grounded circuit fault: power is shorted to ground before the switch, causing lack of control over the power. This is often demonstrated as a light that should not be on, but is.

Some electrical faults cause the fuse to blow. Until the fault is found and rectified, this will continue to happen. The most common reasons for a fuse blowing are: a short circuit; insulation around the wire getting worn or trapped, leading to the copper being exposed, again shorting out; and component failure. Even a bulb blowing can trigger the fuse to blow.

Check areas such as underneath the fuel tank, seat, or even the headlamp shell – these are all places that can trap a wire, causing it to break down and short circuit.

Look out for wires worn through by constant abrasion in areas where there are moving parts. Check around the handlebars, wheels, and chain. If a wire is not routed correctly it could be rubbing and worn through, leading to failure.

When taking parts off your bike, pull the connectors apart one by one to check them. Once a connector is apart, clean the terminals with a little wet or dry paper to get down to the metal. Most connectors will have built up a patina over the years, leading to bad connections. If you clean the terminal whenever you remove or replace a part, by the end of your project you will have cleaned all the connectors, and shouldn't have future problems with wiring.

Ensure that the push fit connectors fit firmly. Many become loose and need to be squeezed tight so they fit snugly again. The same applies to the fuse holders – often these are either dirty or do not hold the fuse tightly enough.

Check the wiring for bad repairs, such as poorly crimped connectors, badly used scotch locks, and joints that are simply wound together with insulating tape. If you find what looks like insulating tape, it is a good idea to remove it completely and check the quality of the repair underneath.

There are two tools that can help you diagnose almost any electrical problem: a multi-meter and a test light. A test light is nothing more than a 12-volt light with a positive and negative lead that allows you to quickly and easily check for power in a circuit. If there is no power, there is no light – simple. Great for checking for breaks in wires. The multi-meter can also do this, but it has numerous other functions. It can check continuity, measure

CLASSIC MOTORCYCLE RESTORATION

10.1 Multi-meters are inexpensive, and invaluable when working on electrics.

10.2 A modern sealed 12V gel battery. These are low maintenance, and do not need to be topped-up with de-ionised water like older batteries.

resistance and amperage, and check for bad grounds.

As with any piece of equipment, read the instructions that came with the multi-meter before attempting to use it on a motorcycle.

If you are planning a long journey, along with your basic bike toolkit I would recommend packing the following for electrical repairs:

Insulating tape
Spare bulbs, in bubble wrap for protection
Combination wire cutters/strippers/crimpers
An assorted selection of solder-less crimp connectors
Spare fuses
Small cable ties (also known as tie wraps)
12VDC test light
A copy of the bike's wiring diagram

THE BATTERY

The battery is the heart of a motorcycle's electrical system, just like the oil is the blood of the engine. It not only releases and stores electricity as needed, but also provides an important role as a 'shock absorber' for voltage spikes and current surges. Properly maintained, a good quality battery will give years of service.

The vast majority of modern motorcycles batteries are now sealed, maintenance-free units. Here are a few simple preventative measures to keep your battery working well and lasting a long time.

Invest in a decent battery optimiser type charger! These are quite cheap nowadays, and will monitor the battery and charge it as needed while it is being stored.

If you intend to store your bike for more than a month, remove the battery and keep it on one of these chargers. For the winter storage, the best thing to do is remove the battery and place it in a cool, dry area, and charge it up once a month at the very least.

Avoid leaving your motorcycle running at idle for long periods. Most motorcycles don't have enough output from their charging systems at idle to charge the battery and run the bike until the revs are up, so you are actually draining the battery slowly when idling.

WIRING DIAGRAMS

When it comes to troubleshooting electrical problems, the most useful tool to have is a proper electrical wiring diagram of your motorcycle. These can usually be found in the workshop manual. Read it and become familiar with it, and the time spent hunting electrical problems will be much reduced.

Remember, an un-insulated live wire can cause a fire!

Generally I like to keep the cost of restorations to a reasonable level, but sometimes the overall condition of the wiring is so bad that it warrants investment in a complete new wiring loom. If you find that there is not one available for your bike, there are places that will make them. Often looms are in subsections, so you may only need one section, but if you opt for a completely new wiring loom rebuild – and providing you have a wiring diagram – a knowledgeable car/bike electrician will be able to make it for you.

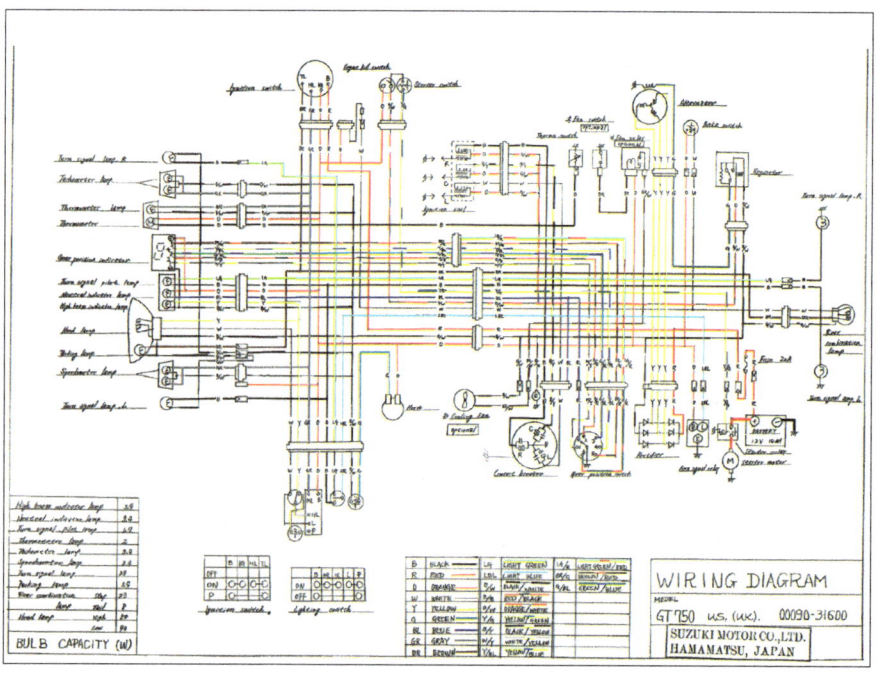

10.3 A typical colour wiring diagram. (Courtesy Suzuki)

ELECTRICS

10.4 What a mess. Poor wiring with makeshift repairs will give endless problems.

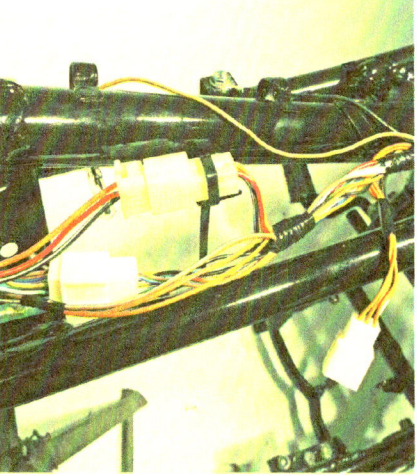

10.6 This is what the wiring should look like once fitted: well spread out and nice clean connectors, with no broken wires.

10.7 Clean the terminals inside all bulb holders, and check all earth connections.

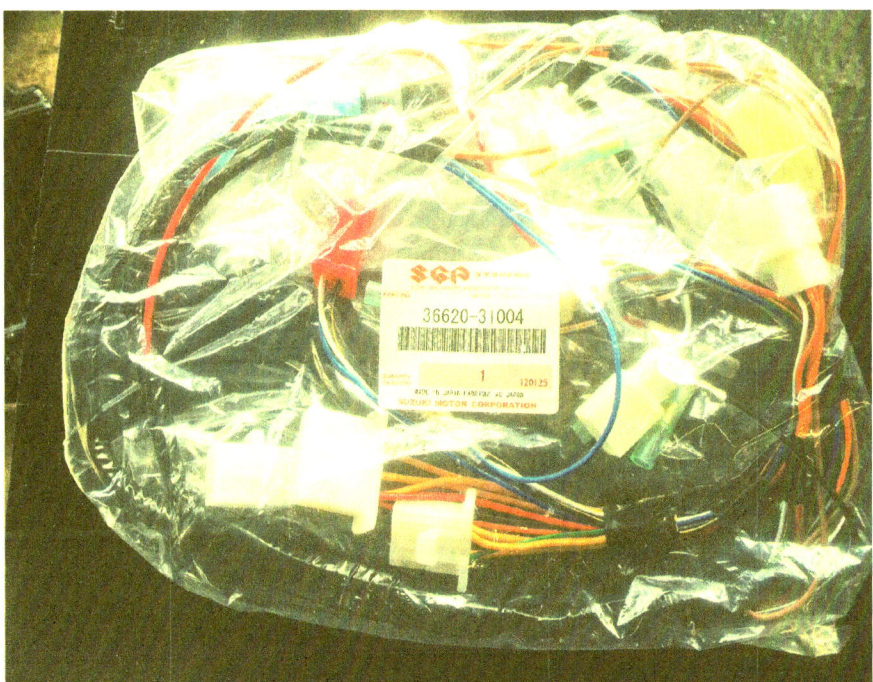

10.5 A brand new loom guarantees trouble-free electrics for the years to come. Luckily, a genuine loom for a 1976 Suzuki was still available when I carried out this project. New wiring gives peace of mind, and confidence that the electrics will not fail on a ride, maybe miles from home.

10.8 This bulb holder also doubled up as a homemade test lamp. Ideal when checking basic connection faults, or when manually setting the contact breaker points on your ignition.

CLASSIC MOTORCYCLE RESTORATION

10.9 The most common fault on electrical circuits is a bad earth (ground), particularly if the frame has just been sprayed or powder-coated. Remove the earth leads, clean with wet and dry paper until bright, and also clean paint from the frame where the earth lead is bolted. This will give a solid earth connection.

10.11 The contact breaker points, or 'points' as they are commonly known, are the most common cause of ignition problems on classic motorcycles. If the gap that the points are to open is not set correctly, the engine will run poorly or not at all, so at the very least clean the points and check the gap. The points gap is set according to the workshop manual.

10.10 Remember: before you spend hours troubleshooting electrics, check the fuse. Although an obvious step, it is sometimes overlooked. Keep some spare fuses in your side panel or under your seat for emergencies.

10.12 Check whether the points are pitted. The continuous spark jumping across the gap causes the surface of the points to erode (pit), as in the picture above. These points will never be set correctly, and need renewing.

IGNITION SYSTEMS

On the ignition side, most classic motorcycles have a battery, ignition coil, contact breaker points, and condensers, finishing with the sparkplug, although some later models do have electronic ignition that needs little or no maintenance other than keeping the ignition timing set accurately. Thankfully, all these parts are replaceable, and generally reasonably priced.

Points are such an important part of your ignition system, and inexpensive to buy. I would always recommend fitting a new set on your restoration. They are freely available, easy to fit, and give a long service, guaranteeing trouble-free operation.

ELECTRICS

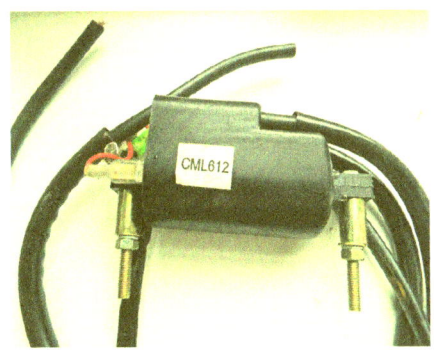

10.15 The final part of your ignition system is the HT coil. If this is faulty, it has to be replaced. It is solid state, and not serviceable. Mostly hidden underneath the fuel tank, it doesn't usually give problems, even after years of use.

10.13 Here, you can see three sets of new contact breaker points with condensers. Note the small piece of felt. This should have a couple of drops of light oil applied to lubricate the cam a little.

10.14 Always fit a new set of sparkplugs. Much attention is given to setting the ignition timing and the points gap, but if the sparkplugs are in poor condition all your efforts setting them won't give you an engine that runs properly.

10.16 The sparkplug HT caps should be changed if there are any cracks. These simply screw into the end of the HT lead.

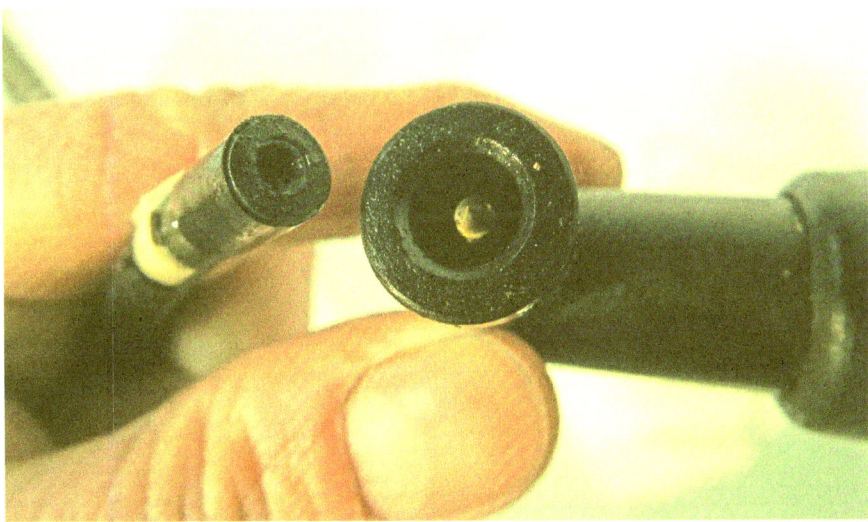

10.17 Check that the screw in the HT cap makes a good connection with the HT wire inside the HT lead. No connection, no spark. You can snip off a small piece of the end of the lead if the screw does not reach the wire, but be careful not to cut off too much, as this could make the lead too short to reach the sparkplug.

81

CLASSIC MOTORCYCLE RESTORATION

CHARGING & STARTING SYSTEMS

Other than the brushes on the starter motor and stator rotor, these two systems are not serviceable. If you do have a fault, the faulty item will need replacing.

It has to be said that these parts generally have a long life, and it is rare to have problems with them. However, the parts of the electrical systems that are most commonly replaced are set out here.

10.18 If you have problems with an electric starter, the starter motor solenoid could be at fault. This is sited between the starter motor and the battery. When the starter button is pressed, the solenoid should click. If it doesn't, test it according to the workshop manual. One simple check is to ensure it is earthed properly.

10.20 The voltage regulator takes a varying voltage and regulates it to a fixed voltage. Short circuits can cause problems with the regulator. If problems are suspected, refer to the workshop manual.

10.19 The indicator flasher unit needs changing if you have problems with indicators (assuming everything else is okay). Below the flasher unit is the rectifier unit. If you have a dead battery or one that discharges quickly, it could point to the rectifier. Again, refer to the workshop manual.

10.21 The alternator stator is not serviceable, except for the carbon brushes which can be replaced. On this engine they are located in the black box on the left, held in by two crosshead screws. The brushes on this model are soldered in place.

ELECTRICS

10.22 The starter motor also has brushes, and it is not a difficult job to replace them.

10.24 These starter motor brushes are held down by coil springs. Replace the brushes if they are worn below the size given in the workshop manual – in this case, 10mm.

10.23 Undo the two screws and remove the starter housing end to get access to the brushes.

10.25 The copper will almost certainly be covered in black carbon dust. Clean with white spirit until it is bright and shiny.

Chapter 11
Spraying, decals & badges

Many parts on a new project were originally painted or lacquered. These parts will almost certainly be scratched, or at the very least have faded over the years. In this chapter we go through the process of respraying these parts and restoring them to their original finish.

11.1 This Yamaha RD350 has great paintwork and decals, showing what can be achieved by respraying. The tank and side panels are easily noticeable, but parts such as headlamp brackets and fork leg covers are often forgotten.

Parts that are usually painted or powder-coated:
Fuel tank
Side panels
Frame
Swinging arm
Side and main stand
Footrest brackets
Top and bottom yokes
Rear torque arm
Battery compartment
Air filter box
Fork ears (headlamp brackets)
Fork leg shrouds
Headlamp cowl
Brake callipers
Speedo and tachometer housing
Seat base
Handlebar switchgear
Engine mounting brackets

You can see that a considerable number of parts need painting if you want your bike to look as good as new. The preparation and painting are the same whatever you are intending to respray. If the part you are painting or spraying has decals attached, have a proper look where they are placed: you may want to take a photo to refer to later on. It may also be useful to take measurements of the current decals.

Firstly, remember spray fumes from thinners and paints are dangerous and highly flammable. For the same reason, pack paints should only be used by professionals with the appropriate safety equipment although it is more durable and can be polished to a higher shine than other paints. Aerosol and cellulose paints are more suitable for DIY use. Do not use near flames or sparks, and wear the appropriate face mask at all times. Speak to your paint provider if you are not sure which mask to use.

Likewise, when sanding use an appropriate dust particle mask as sanding dust can damage your health.

TOOLS AND MATERIALS

11.2 A wide range of paint shop products are needed to complete your project. Because of the small size of motorcycle parts, spray cans can produce a good result if you do not have spray equipment.

SPRAYING, DECALS & BADGES

Preparation
Sander, filler, cellulose putty, wet or dry paper grades 120, 240, 500, dust particle mask, degreaser.

Priming
Spray aerosol primer or compressor and spray gun, primer, thinners, tack cloth, spray mask. Strainer if you are using a spray gun.

Finish coat
The same tools that you used when priming, finish paint, 1200 grade wet or dry paper, and polishing compound.

Let's start with the fuel tank. This is often the main focus of attention, and must look good.

Once the tank is cleaned inside and completely empty of fuel, as described in chapter nine, remove the fuel tap, cap, and all badges or decals, so that you have a completely bare tank.

Since this is a beginner's book, I will assume you are using spray cans. There are many paint suppliers that mix the colour you require and send it in an aerosol, because the area that needs spraying on a motorcycle is relatively small, and does not always justify buying spray equipment. If you do have spray equipment, the process is the same.

STRIPPING PAINT
Preparation is paramount, and is reflected in the finished paint surface quality. With major parts in a very bad condition – for instance a fuel tank – it is worth spending the extra time stripping it back to the bare metal (do not use paint stripper on any part that is plastic). Preparing for painting over badly adhering paint may take just as long, and results will be far from perfect.

Chemical strippers are very strong, so follow the manufacturer's safety instruction. Gloves, goggles, and good ventilation are essential.

The process for stripping parts is shown from picture 11.4 on.

Next wash the part thoroughly with water (this neutralises the stripper) and dry it.

Use a two-part car body filler to fix dents. Follow the instructions, smoothing the filler into the dent, leaving it slightly proud of the tank surface.

11.3 There are automotive paint strippers available for removing old paint from car body panels. These are suitable on any of the metal parts you need to paint.

11.4 Lightly brush the stripper onto the part that needs to be stripped. After a short while the paint will start to bubble and blister. Once the entire part has been covered with stripper, begin to scrape off the paint with a paint scraper.

If the dent is large, build up one or two layers of filler. Once you have all the dents filled, let the filler harden. When completely hardened, begin to sand the filled areas (use a dust mask and goggles here) with wet and dry abrasive paper. Begin with a reasonably coarse grade of 120 just to get the shape. Use a rubber sanding block if you find it easier. Keep the paper wrapped around. Once you have sanded to the shape required, go over again with progressively finer and finer grades of wet and dry. After grade 120, use 240, 500, and finish with 1200. Ensure you keep the wet and dry paper wet when sanding. This helps keep the paper from being clogged up with old paint residue.

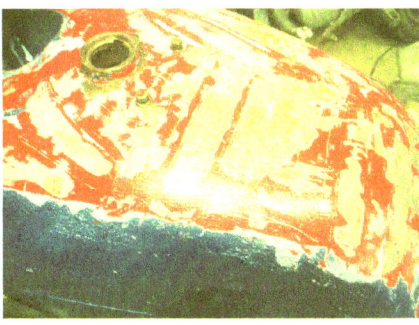

11.5 This will remove almost all of the paint. Some difficult-to-reach areas may need another coat, and you can get in the tiny corners by using a small wire brush or some wire wool.

11.6 Once the part is dry, take a closer look. If there are any dents, these should be filled to restore the tank to its original shape.

11.7 This tank has been completely sanded, with dents filled. Dry thoroughly and spray the first coat of primer. Spraying should only be carried out in a well-ventilated area, wearing the appropriate safety mask goggles. Spray fumes should not be inhaled. Follow the instructions on the can.

CLASSIC MOTORCYCLE RESTORATION

11.8 A tank rubbed down after the first primer coat.

11.10 Once you have applied a few coats of primer you will begin to see small imperfections that still need to be filled and rubbed down.

11.11 Use fine surface body filler and go over these with a fine wet and dry sandpaper, keeping it wet until the area is smooth again. Now apply two more coats of primer.

11.9 Find a solid platform on which to place the part to be sprayed, or, better still, hang the tank on a piece of strong cord or wire like this swing arm is. This will allow you to spray all sides, on top, and underneath without moving it.

If you can't hang the tank, spray the underneath first, and once it is completely dry turn it over and spray the top and sides. Ensure the primer and finish paint are completely dry between coats. If the paint is still slightly wet and you apply more, runs will occur, which you'll have to rub out.

Continue this process until there are no imperfections and the tank is completely smooth and fully primed.

If you come across very small scratches or dents, use more fine filler or cellulose putty. This is applied lightly with a small plastic spatula and pressed into the scratches or dents, and usually dries quite quickly.

Now that you have the tank 100% smooth and fully primed, move onto the finish coats.

Carefully wipe the tank using a tack cloth to remove any fine dust from the area to be sprayed.

If you are happy with the results, pat yourself on the back, well done. It's not easy the first time, and if you have

SPRAYING, DECALS & BADGES

11.12 A scratch filled with fine cellulose putty.

11.13 Spray two or three coats of finish paint, letting it dry completely between coats. Take a look at it. Has it picked up any dust while spraying? Are there any runs? Does the paint look a little like orange peel texture? Any of these will mean another rub over with a fine grade wet and dry paper.

After a few attempts you will have a finished tank with no blemishes. If the paint is metallic, follow up with two coats of lacquer to get the final shine. Lacquer can also be flattened and polished, but, as with the top coat, wait until the lacquer has hardened fully.

Once the last coats have hardened, whether it is lacquer or paint, go over the entire tank with a fine rubbing compound or 2000 grit paper and a soft block until you have a high shine.

Whenever you rub down or polish, ensure the surface is completely free from any particles that could scratch the finished work.

Once the spraying is finished, turn your attention to the badges and decals, to finish off the appearance of your bike.

DECALS

All motorcycles have decals. Some are decorative, eg pin striping, and others are for information, such as tyre pressure and safety warning stickers. To make your bike look as original as possible, try to locate the decals for your model. Some are still available from manufactures, but many are discontinued. However, help is at hand. There are many decal companies that reproduce exact copies of originals.

11.14 The side panels and fork leg shrouds, all painted the same as the tank.

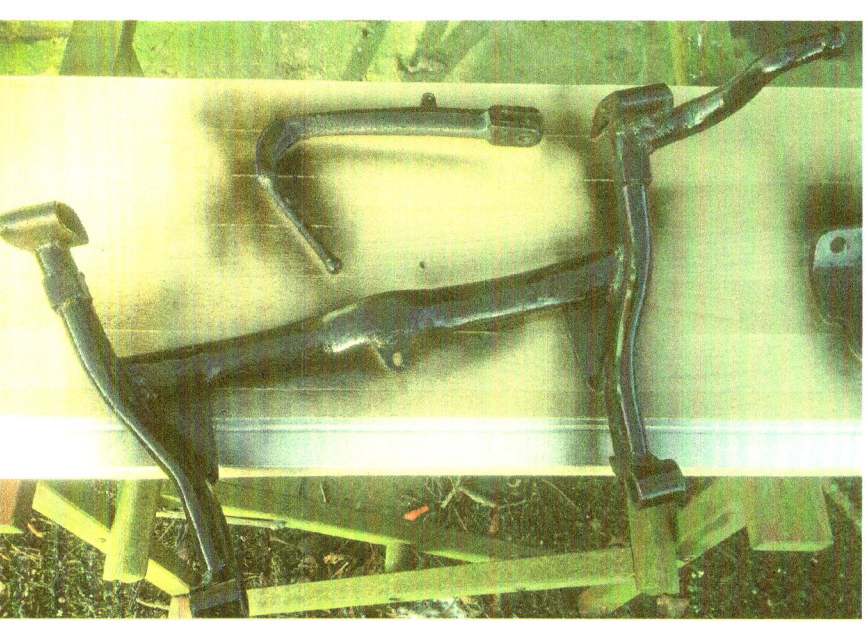

11.15 Don't forget to paint the smaller parts of your project, such as the stands and brackets.

a good result now, results will only get better in the future.

Don't worry too much if it is not 100%. It's your first attempt. Runs, dust and the orange peel effect are common, and can all be dealt with. If you do have runs, lightly rub down the affected areas and respray.

If you have the orange peel effect, this can be flattened with a very fine, wet and dry paper once the paint has cured. Leave as long as recommended by the manufacturer. The paint needs to be hard before you begin cutting back.

CLASSIC MOTORCYCLE RESTORATION

11.16 A variety of sticker decals for a Honda CB400F.

Most decals are small stickers that peel off a backing paper and are simply stuck to the bike. With vinyl decals the technique is more involved, and can be quite challenging to get right.

There are two main methods of applying decals: the wet method, and the dry method. Both are basically the same procedure, but the wet method gives a little more time for final positioning of the decal.

The main rules
Do a practice run first, positioning the decal without sticking it, so you have a basic idea where it will go.

Relax, take your time. If you rush you will make mistakes

Here are the tools required:
Craft knife
Small garden sprayer
Lint free cloth

11.17 The stripes don't look much to begin with. They come either folded or rolled up. Unfold/unroll them and place on a flat surface, which helps them return to original shape, and prevents them lifting when being put on.

11.18 Try and find a fixed point to measure from. If you cannot find one, use a piece of card as seen here. This gives a fixed point that can be transferred to the tank when you are ready to put on the stripes.

SPRAYING, DECALS & BADGES

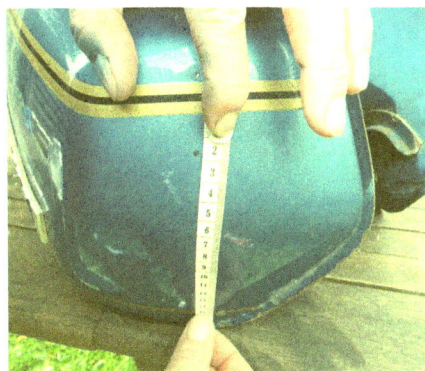

11.19 If you have more than one stripe, measure the distance between them and note all the measurements.

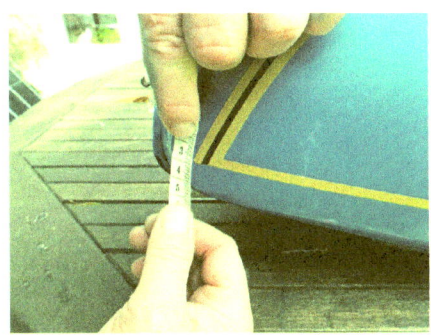

11.20 Take plenty of measurements. The more you take, the more accurate the new stripe will be.

Before you remove the backing paper, cut it as close to the decal as you can, being sure not to damage the decal.
Add two drops of washing-up liquid to the garden sprayer, then fill with cold water. Lightly spray the solution onto the tank.

11.21 Lightly spray the tank with water and position the stripes gently on the tank. Then, with a pencil, make small marks on the tank to highlight the points measured. This will help keep the decal in the right position.

Next, remove the backing paper from the decal, and carefully stick the decal onto the tank using the pencil lines as a guide. Press the decal firmly all over, being careful not to stretch or scratch it.

11.22 Lastly, peel off the top layer of paper to reveal the finished stripe.

11.23 Wipe with a lint-free cloth to dry the area.

11.24 If you have two stripes, overlap them at the corner and trim with a craft knife to a clean edge.

CLASSIC MOTORCYCLE RESTORATION

11.25 That's it. You have just applied your own decal. More money saved. With a couple of coats of lacquer, this tank will look like new.

BADGES

Badges, like decals, are a way for the manufactures to really get across their marketing message. Badges such as Twin-cam, GT and Super Sport are all designed to get us, the customer, interested, and they advertise the main features of the motorcycle.

A set of badges in original condition can fetch a good price on auction websites, because they are becoming more and more difficult to find in good condition.

Some reproductions are available, but are often of poor quality. I know of some that didn't fit the locating holes on the side panels, leaving the buyer to cut off the locating pins and glue the badge in position. This is not what you should be doing having just paid good money for a new part.

You can have some success restoring badges, particularly if they are metal or alloy.

11.26 This is one of my favourite badges from a Honda CB350 Four. Badges on modern motorcycles are often really only decals. But on some classics, they were much more elaborate and decorative, mostly made of metal, alloy, or plastic. Raised embossed types are very attractive.

11.27 All resprayed with decals and badges applied, and looking very smart.

Chapter 12
Clocks & switches

The clocks and switches on your motorcycle almost always need refurbishing. The paint will be worn, flaky, and pretty dull at best. The surrounds on the clock are most likely rusty around the edges, and the dial faces could be faded by the sun after years of exposure.

Let's begin by looking at the switchgear. Give it a general first assessment. Do the switches still move? Are they complete, with all switch covers and buttons in place? Are all the wires there? And are the connectors present?

Once you have the switchgear off the bike, find a clean space on your work bench. Some of the parts in the gear are very small, so you need good lighting. Springs are a particular problem, so be careful when pulling apart the switchgear.

Take a few photos as you proceed. It is easy to strip the gear, but if you haven't made a record or taken a few pictures, it may be difficult to remember where all the small pieces go.

Most workshop manuals do not show a detailed stripdown of the switchgear, so it is up to you to remember where everything goes.

12.1 A Suzuki switchgear in bad condition. Switches missing and bent, with paint peeling.

12.3 Disconnect the wiring connector. This is usually hidden in the headlamp shell.

12.2 Unscrew the two screws holding together the halves of the switchgear. Look out for any broken pieces or springs that may fall out.

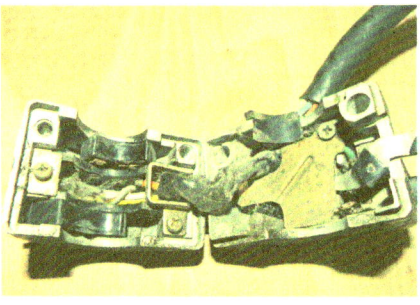

12.4 With the switchgear on the bench open the switch body. It is probably full of dirt and cobwebs. Carefully dismantle and remove all the internal parts from the main body.

CLASSIC MOTORCYCLE RESTORATION

12.5 Once dismantled, the switchgear looks like this. Be sure to use the correct screwdriver on these tiny screws. They are not very forgiving, and will round off very quickly if you use the wrong size. The correct size screwdriver and a firm hold will crack the join between the head of the screw and the body, and the screw will come out cleanly. Remove all the screws and put somewhere safe – a small plastic container dedicated to each switch is a good idea. Try not to mix up the screws and springs between different switchgears.

If you want your bike to look as it did when first built, check whether your switches should be gloss, matt, or semi-matt paint finished. One small aerosol can paint many switches, with three coats for paint. Follow the instructions on the can – three coats are usually sufficient.

Once the paint has dried, move on to painting the letters. This is a fiddly task, but worth undertaking.

Use a small paint brush and the correct colour paint from a hobby model shop. I find it easier to paint the lettering then wipe off the excess. It is almost impossible to paint the letters without the orange (in this case) getting on the newly painted black body.

12.8 Paint with a small brush, then wipe off the excess.

Now that everything is apart, give it all a thorough clean. Degrease the copper contact parts, and use some fine wet and dry paper to remove the patina from the contact areas. Sand lightly until the metal is bright again.

Blow out the dust from inside the now-empty switchgear body, and clean the entire thing, including small parts, in warm soapy water, and dry thoroughly. Everything should now look about as good as you can get it before putting it all back together again.

This is the time to repaint the body while everything is still apart: the best opportunity to do so, and there will be no masking.

Paint the letters, trying not to get too much colour on the black, then wipe off the excess paint before it has time to dry.

12.6 Sand the old paint until smooth with some medium 240 wet and dry paper, or, if you have a blast cabinet, sandblast off the paint completely. I use a blast cabinet now, but for years did a perfectly good job restoring switches simply sanding them by hand.

12.7 A semi-matt finish. These switch bodies were painted outside to ensure good ventilation.

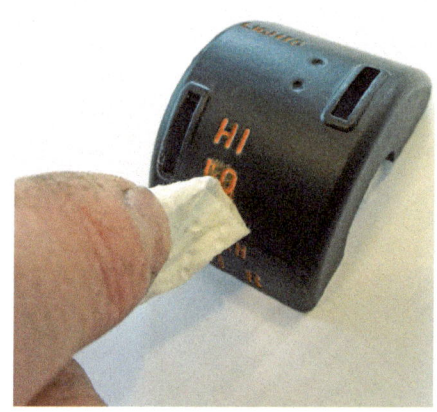

12.9 Wiping off excess paint.

CLOCKS & SWITCHES

You may need to apply more than one coat. Let it dry and check the results. If you are happy with it, you can now rebuild the switchgear, ready to go back on the bike at a later date.

12.10 The letters after just one coat of paint. Looking good already.

When putting everything back together, apply a small amount of grease to any parts that might wear. Be careful not to get grease on the copper contact parts.

There is usually a correct order to how everything should go back together. If you have taken photos while dismantling, it will be easier to rebuild.

To give you an idea what to look out for when rebuilding the switchgear, follow these photographic steps for reassembling a Suzuki part. Other manufacturers are likely to use the same principles.

Picture 12.11 shows the horn button in place with the spring visible. Inside the spring is a small copper pin that, when the horn button is pressed, touches the other part of the switch inside. You can see the two locating slots in which the other part of the horn switch sits.

Picture 12.12 shows the slot-in second part of the horn switch. The slot should be facing downwards, so the copper pin can slip into it when the part is pushed into place. If this part is upside down, the second part of the switch will either fail the copper

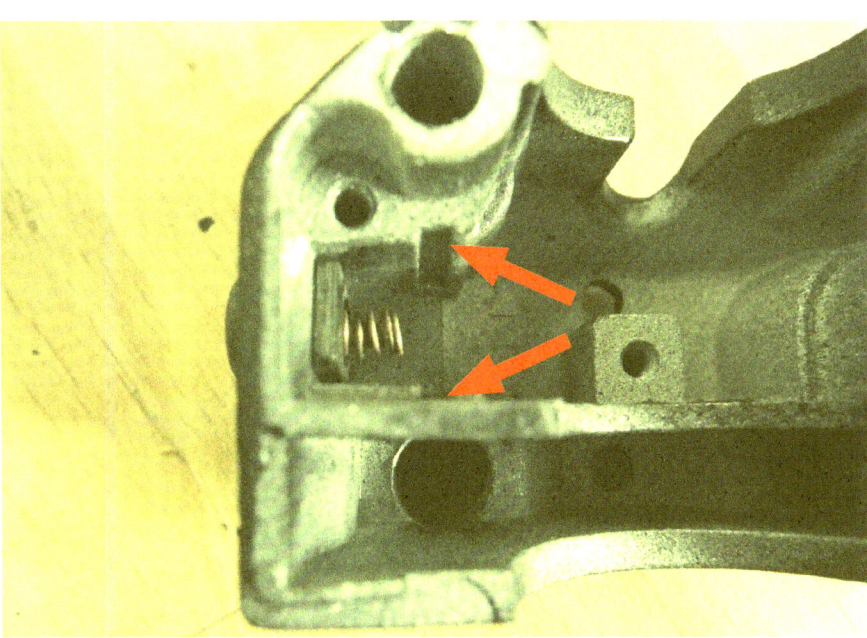

12.11. Be careful not to lose the tiny springs. Note the two positioning slots, which hold the other part of the horn switch.

12.12 The second part of the horn switch, showing the small slot that the copper pin fits into. This slot should face downward as shown.

pin and break it, or just won't slot into place at all. Bear in mind that these parts are old and brittle, and should not be forced into place. If you try to force these little parts, they simply break.

In picture 12.13 the switch is now complete, with both parts correctly in place.

12.13 The horn button complete, with both parts in place.

93

CLASSIC MOTORCYCLE RESTORATION

Once the switch is back in place, secure it and the cable with the brass holders. This part of the switch is now rebuilt.

12.14 The switch and wires secured in place with the holder.

Here are a couple more examples of positioning internal parts.

12.15 The black tab locates into a slot in the switchgear body.

12.16 The slot where the black tab goes, holding the switch securely.

Keep a lookout for this type of positioning guidance on your switchgear. It helps everything go back together nicely and work properly when finished.

12.17 The switchgear rebuilt and repainted, looking like new.

CLOCKS AND GAUGES

Just like the switchgear, the clocks and gauges can be brought back to reasonable condition quite easily and cheaply if you are carrying out a general cosmetic overhaul. I won't go into the internal workings of the speedometer or tachometer, because if either of these don't work it is much easier to find a replacement than to repair.

Generally speaking, clocks and gauges still work okay even after long periods of inactivity, and it is only the dial faces, paintwork, and maybe glass that need attention.

If the dial face has faded, either live with it or attempt to change it. This depends on how bad the fading is, and how good you would like the overall finish to be.

Dial faces for most motorcycles are available online. Fitting these mean stripping the clocks, many of which were not designed to be taken apart. The biggest problem is that a lot of them have a pressed steel band around the clock base, holding it together.

12.18 These Suzuki clocks are suffering from exposure to the Colorado sun, and need a cosmetic makeover.

CLOCKS & SWITCHES

12.19 If the dial face is still in an acceptable condition, don't take apart the clock. Masking the glass and chrome ring and simply respraying the clock is the best approach, as dismantling and rebuilding it is not always successful. Here I have used a craft knife to cut the masking tape as close to the edge as possible.

If you do dismantle the clock, the procedure is set out from picture 12.20 on.

12.20 Gently prise up the edge of the chrome ring all the way around until it can be lifted from the clock. Be very patient when doing this, and be careful not to damage the chrome ring, as it will be impossible to rebuild the clock.

12.21 Before the housing can be removed, unscrew this tiny screw and remove the milometer knob.

12.22 The speedo and tacho needles simply prise off.

12.23 Remove the faceplate screws.

CLASSIC MOTORCYCLE RESTORATION

12.24 Unscrew the bolts at the back and remove the chrome cover.

12.27 The inner housing does not require painting, and really only supports the glass.

12.25 Once the housing is off, remove the glass and prepare the housing for painting.

12.28 Clean the glass before putting it back on the inner housing. Note the rubber seal.

12.26 The clock housing is in three parts.

12.29 The outer housing is then placed over the top of the glass.

CLOCKS & SWITCHES

12.32 Polish the chrome backing and refit to the clock.

12.30 Stick on the new dial face and replace the screws and needle.
TIP! Position the new dial face over the old face before you take off the backing, and with a small pin, make holes where the two screws go. This helps locate the dial face in exactly the right position.

12.33 The tachometer with the new dial face in place, ready to be put on the bike.

12.31 The most difficult task is refitting the chrome band. This should be repositioned and gently squeezed with a set of pliers all around, until it is tight and holding together the clock again. This is a delicate job, and care should be taken not to damage the ring. If you do not get this part right it is unlikely the clock will ever go back together. In the case of the speedo, remember to put the milometer knob back on.

12.34 Clocks finished and refitted to the bike.

Chapter 13
Seat

Almost all restoration projects have problems with the rider's seat. The constant change between cold and warm weather conditions over a long period of time, or being leant up against a wall or shed, causes the cover to split or tear. On a finished project it is essential that the seat looks and feels right.

Seats can be recovered, and if the splits/tears are not too large, the foam underneath may be in useable condition.

Foam is an easy material to work with, and if you have only a small repair it is quite simple to cut a piece

13.2 The worst problem you could have on a seat is with the seat base itself. Most seats have pressed metal bases that rust over the years, and a badly corroded base can often be irreparable. The hinges and brackets need to be sound and firmly fixed to the base. If they don't have a good fixing, look at a way of repairing the base.

13.1 It is not often that the foam is completely unusable, but if it has been exposed to sunlight, ultraviolet light causes it to deteriorate, making it unusable.

and place it into a damaged area with a little glue. However, foam that has been exposed for too long is not repairable, and completely new seat foam will be required. The seat cover, when fitted, is tight and helps hold the repair in place.

Seat covers are available for almost all motorcycles, and are not difficult to fit.

If the seat cover is in need of renewal, ensure that you order the exact cover for your motorcycle model, year, and type. I once ordered a seat cover for a Honda 1973 CB350T, which was slightly different from my model, a 1973 CB350F. I had to buy a second cover after the first one tore while I was trying to 'Make it fit.' Lesson learnt.

SEAT

13.3 A seat base like this is too badly corroded to be repaired. You can see that the edge has completely rusted away. If there are only small holes these can be covered by a plate riveted over, returning some strength to that area, but more serious damage means another seat is needed.

13.4 This seat base is in good condition, showing only light rust. It is complete with all hinges and catches, which are solidly attached to the seat base. Also visible are the seat rubbers that support the seat on the motorcycle frame. There are six rubbers on this seat.

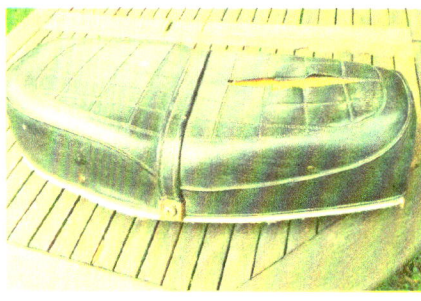

13.5 This seat needs to be recovered to return it to useable condition; luckily it has only a minimal amount of foam damage.

13.6 The chrome-look edge trim is badly worn, and the lettering very faded.

15.7 The seat has metal clasps and hooks all around the inside edge of the base. These hold the seat cover tightly in place. Often, these clasps are broken or rusted away. This clasp is in good condition.

99

CLASSIC MOTORCYCLE RESTORATION

13.8 Begin by unbolting all the brackets and hinges ready for degreasing and painting.

13.11 If your seat has a strap fitted, remove it to allow the seat cover to come off.

13.9 Once the brackets and hinges are removed, gently pull back all the clasps with a pair of pliers. Do not bend too far – just enough to clear the seat edge trim.

13.12 Some of these screws are very tight, and you may have to use a more forceful method of removal. This screw would not budge easily, and a new one had to be found. This method is likely to damage the screw, but is often the only way to remove it.

13.10 The smaller clasps are not as easy to get at with pliers, so use a flatblade screwdriver or similar to prise them off.

13.13 Pull the edge trim off the seat, working all the way around the seat base until the seat cover can be removed completely.

SEAT

13.14 Pull off the seat cover, being careful not to damage the foam.

13.15 This seat foam is in relatively good condition considering it is 40 years old. It still has a good shape, and there is only minor foam damage where the cover tear was.

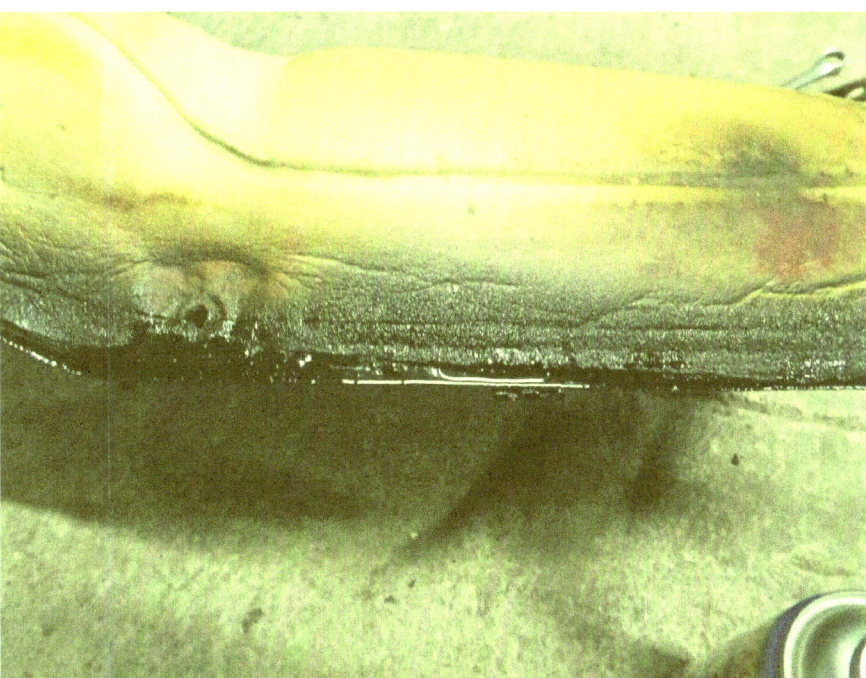

13.17 Paint or spray the edge once the rust is removed. This gives a clean surface for the edge trim to stick to.

13.18 Place the cover loosely over the foam base.

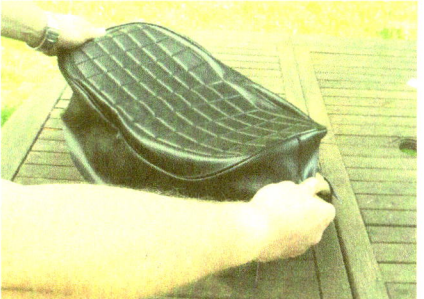

13.16 Clean the seat base edge to remove any rust. The edge trim uses glue, and needs a sound surface to adhere to.

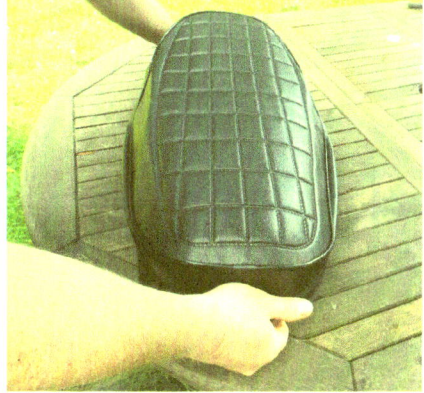

13.19 Pull the front and back of the cover so that the seat cover edging lines up with the seat's profile. Do this on both sides, so the seat pattern is central to the seat top.

CLASSIC MOTORCYCLE RESTORATION

Original seat edge trim is almost impossible to find. However there is an effective alternative. Car door edging is inexpensive, and very effective in giving an almost original trim look to a seat.

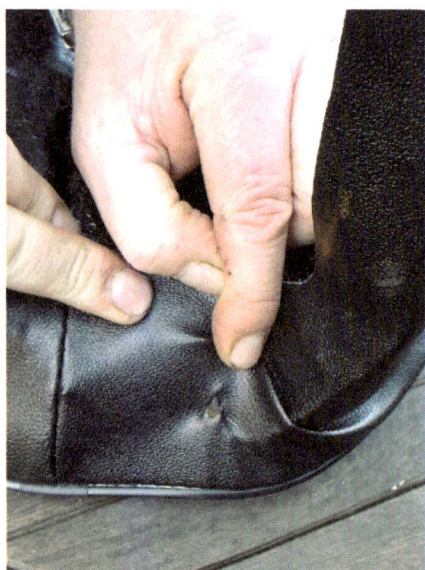

13.20 With the cover pulled tightly at the front, pierce with the pointed clasps.

13.23 If you cannot find the correct seat edging, use car door trim to achieve an acceptable result.

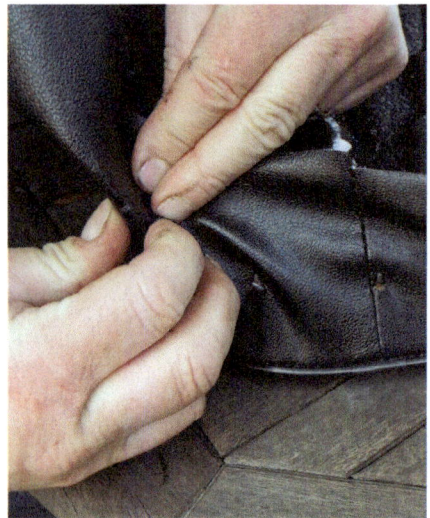

13.21 Work across the front of the seat until all the pointed clasps are through, and bend them so that they hold the seat cover in position.

13.22 Do the same at the back and all around the edge with the bigger clasps.

13.24 The car door edge trim is open at the bottom and inside is filled with glue.

SEAT

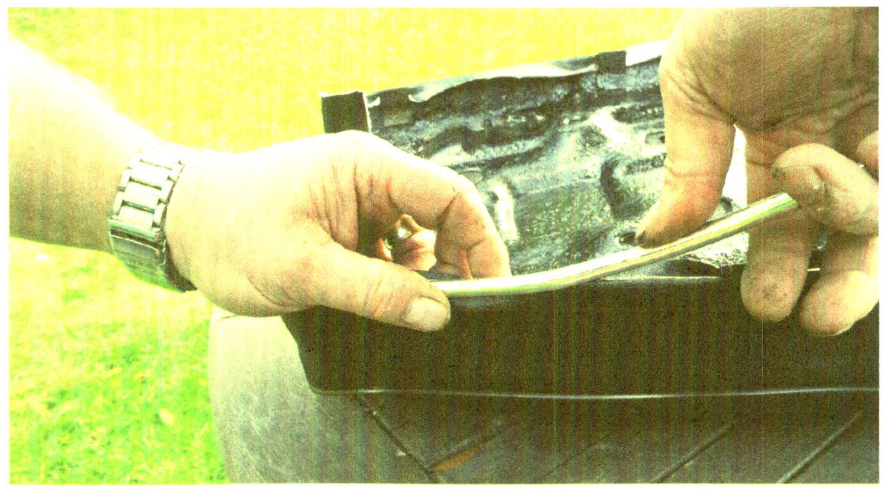

13.25 Begin on one of the front corners, pushing the trim over the edge of the seat until you have gone round to the other corner. Push down firmly – the trim has a tight fit, and will hold the cover tight.

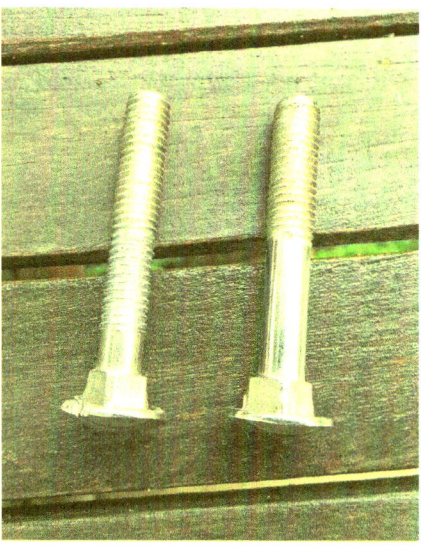

13.30 These stainless steel coach bolts were found, and the thread cut to the full length of the bolt.

13.26 With a sharp pair of scissors, cut the front edge to the same angle as the front of the seat.

13.28 The seat almost finished, looking like new. We just need to add the strap and we're done.

Some parts of your restoration may no longer be available, particularly smaller detail parts. In this case, find an alternative replacement that still gives the original finish and quality.

13.31 The bolt was then cut to the length required and pushed through the folded strap.

13.27 Using a craft knife, trim any excess material under the chrome trim edge. This leaves a nice clean finish.

13.29 Because the original seat strap screws are not available any more, a suitable replacement had to be found.

CLASSIC MOTORCYCLE RESTORATION

13.32 The thread on the original nut (which is welded to the seat base) was damaged; therefore it was drilled out, and a new stainless steel nut used.

13.34 Lettering standing out proud again.

13.33 The finished seat with the strap fitted, looking very respectable.

13.35 A Honda seat sporting the new chrome trim, lettering, and strap.

Chapter 14
Forks

Motorcycle manufacturers have designed various kinds of front suspension. The vast majority are telescopic forks with hydraulic damping, and this chapter covers the stripping and rebuilding of front forks of this kind, since it is the type that you are most likely to come across on your project.

Before attempting to rebuild the front forks, you should check for scratches on the stanchions. Scratches cause damage to the fork oil seal, and in this case the stanchions need to be reground and plated by a specialist company. It is pointless fitting new seals if this hasn't been carried out beforehand – the seal will simply fail again. You still need to strip the forks in order to send the stanchions for refurbishment.

It is common to find that the fork oil has leaked or broken down making it unusable, and in need of replacement. Use the correct grade of oil and top up to the correct level. This is usually a measured amount when filling up the forks.

The main components of the front forks are illustrated in the following photo sequence.

14.1 The fork leg, which will be polished, and is the part that the stanchions slide into. On most motorcycles this leg comprised the bottom part of the forks, although later, mainly on sports models, it was the upper part of the forks. These are known as **USD**, or upside down forks.

14.2 You can see here the drain plug screw. Remove to change the fork oil.

105

CLASSIC MOTORCYCLE RESTORATION

14.3 The stanchion, which is chrome-plated and slides into the fork leg. If this part is scratched it will damage the seal and lead to an oil leak. The stanchion often has a cover in the form of either a rubber gaiter or a painted metal shroud to protect it.

14.6 The sign of a fork leg that is leaking oil. The oil seal needs replacing.

14.4 A close up of the stanchion shows rust and pit marks. This stanchion will need to be reground and chrome-plated before the fork leg can be rebuilt.

14. 7 Drain any oil in the forks. Use the small screw at the bottom of the fork leg, or turn the fork upside down, to pour the oil into a container (not glass). You may have to compress the fork a little to expel oil, which is why we do not use a glass container, which could crack.

14.5 The coil spring can become compressed over time, and needs to be checked against the manufacturer's specifications to determine if it is still the correct useable length. This measurement is found in your workshop manual.

14.8 Remove the dust cover by prising it out of its slot and sliding it off the top of the fork leg.

FORKS

14.9 Now we can see the circlip in the top of the fork leg. Clean off any visible rust.

14.12 This screw is often very tight, and may never before have been removed. It is important to use the correct size screwdriver or Allen key. If this screw/bolt becomes rounded it is very difficult to repair because of its location. Try shocking the screw before attempting to turn it, which helps break the adhesion.

14.10 Holding the leg firmly, remove the circlip and give it a good clean.

14.13 On most motorcycles there is a nut with an O ring seal here. Remove the oil seal, making sure you don't damage the inner face.

14.11 There is a bolt (sometimes a screw) on the underside of the fork leg that should be removed.

14.14 Withdraw the stanchion: sometimes a slide hammer action is needed.

CLASSIC MOTORCYCLE RESTORATION

14.15 Once out, the spring becomes visible. Be prepared for more oil to spill out here.

14.18 Grease the stanchion slightly before refitting the top bush to the forks.

14.16 Clean the damper rod thoroughly.

14.19 Clean the inside of the fork leg, and ensure the seal recess is cleaned properly.

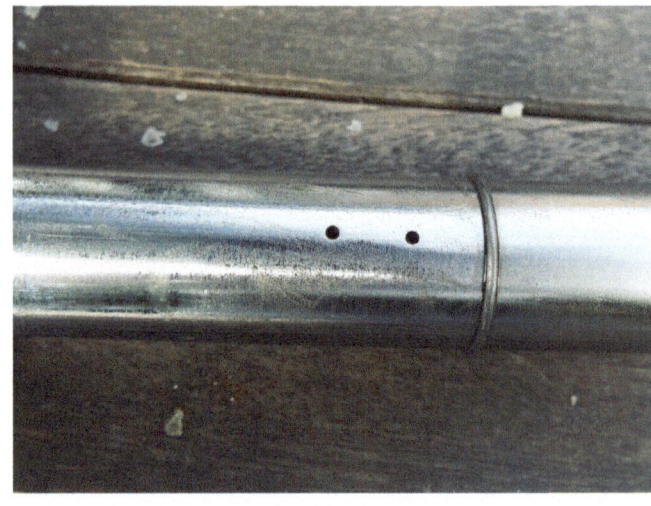

14.17 All visible holes must be clear of debris.

14.20 Fit a new pair of fork seals.

FORKS

14.21 Slide the new seal over the stanchion.

14.24 Slide the stanchion into the leg.

14.22 Replace the damper rod.

14.25 Push it all into the leg far enough to refit the circlip. Once the circlip is in, ensure it sits firmly inside the groove. Now replace the bottom bolt and dust cover.

14.23 Replace the coil spring.

14.26 Finally, fill with fork oil to the level recommended by the manufacturer.

109

Chapter 15
The rebuild

The rebuild can begin once you have the frame, swinging arm and stands repainted/resprayed. Ahead of starting, ensure that all nuts, bolts and washers are as clean as possible, or, if they are to be replaced, you have replacements ready.

Some projects are rebuilt over a long period of time due to the difficulty in finding the parts required. You can still begin the rebuild, and add to the project as parts become available.

FRAME BUILD AND REAR END

15.1 Raise the frame off the floor onto a solid platform to give good support when fitting the stands and swinging arm.

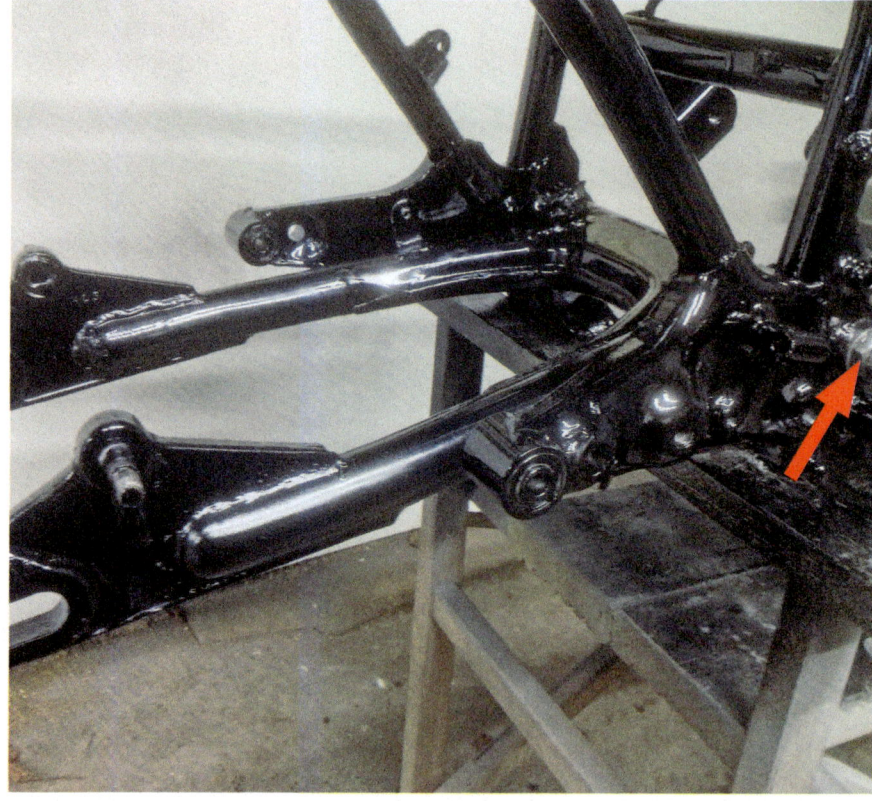

15.2 Fit the swinging arm by tapping the pivot bolt (arrowed) through lightly with a rubber mallet. Be sure to grease the bushes and the large swinging arm bolt, and tighten to the torque setting described in the workshop manual. The swinging arm should now move freely, with no side-to-side play which would indicate worn bushes.

THE REBUILD

15.3 Use a socket or spanner on both ends of the swinging arm pivot bolt to prevent it turning while tightening.

15.5 Fit the stands while the frame is supported. When doing so, slightly grease the eyes where the stand springs clip on.

15.6 Next, fit both rear shock absorbers, making sure that the rubber bushes are in good condition. If dome nuts are not original, use stainless steel dome nuts instead. These nuts are always visible, and using stainless steel replacements enhances the finished appearance.

15.4 If the sidestand has a separate bracket, it can be easier to fit the spring if you place the bracket in a vice and put the spring in place before bolting the stand to the bracket.

15.7 If a rear grab rail was fitted originally, but is not available now, use several washers on the top shock mounting as spacers until you can locate a grab rail.

CLASSIC MOTORCYCLE RESTORATION

15.8 Replace the rear plastic mudguard if the item on your project comes in two pieces.

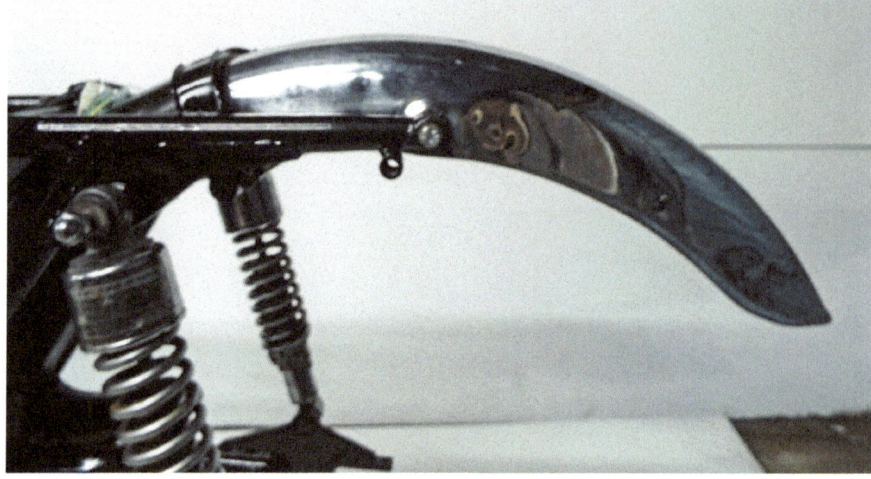

15.11 Once the plastic part of the mudguard is fitted, bolt on the chrome half. This is held on by four bolts. Two are on the rear of the frame as shown here, and two are hidden on the inside of the frame by the top suspension mounting.

15.9 On this model there are two rubbers which push onto the frame before the mudguard can be fitted. Then it simply slots over the rubbers for a snug fit.

15.12 Bolt on the rear light and bracket via four nuts and bolts: two at the top and two underneath at the rear. These are often rubber-mounted, with a small metal sleeve inside.

15.10 Ensure that wires are free and don't become trapped, which may lead to electrical problems later on.

15.13 The seat lock can now be fitted. This is held on by two small bolts. Do not over-tighten these.

112

THE REBUILD

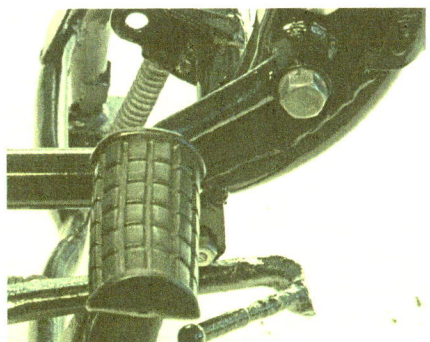

15.14 Depending on make and model, the footrests can be fitted now, or after fitting the exhaust system.

15.15 Some fuel tanks bolt down at the back. On this model an elastic strap is used for quick release.

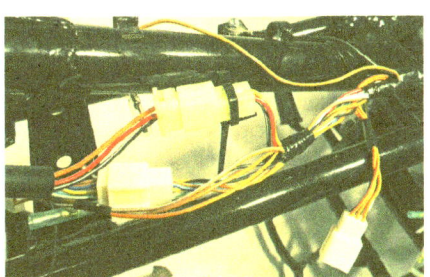

15.16 Fit the wiring loom along the entire length of the frame. If you don't have the original ties, use cable ties and snip off the ends to make them look neater.

15.17 when fitting the electrical component panel, ensure that it earths (grounds) properly to the frame, especially on a newly-coated frame. If the earth connection does not work well, electrical problems are likely.

REBUILDING THE FRONT END

15.18 When fitting the ball bearings, put plenty of grease on the bearing carriers, and ensure the bearings are cleaned and greased before insertion. The grease not only lubricates the bearings, but also prevents them falling out while you are inserting the stem.

15.19 Apply plenty of grease to the carrier on the bottom yoke, too, and place the bearings on the carrier.

CLASSIC MOTORCYCLE RESTORATION

15.20 When inserting the steering stem, ensure no bearings fall out of the carriers. Slide the stem in carefully, trying not to let the top of the stem dislodge the bearings in the top yoke carrier.

15.21 Now fit the dust cover and nut. Screw hand-tight for now.

15.22 Support the stem from below until the dust cover and nut are fitted. Tighten just enough so that there is no up and down movement in the steering stem.

If you are fitting tapper roller bearings, remove the old ball bearing carriers. Use a strong piece of steel rod or similar to tap them out. Fitting the tapper bearings is quite easy, but use a piece of wood placed over the bearing that you gently tap in. Ensure you keep it square. If it begins to go in at an angle, it will jam – they are a very tight fit. Fitting tapper roller bearings can make the fork ears (headlamp brackets) slightly loose due to there being a slight difference in steering stem height, so you may need to put an extra large O ring in to take up the slack.

15.23 Next fit the top yoke (triple clamp) nut and washer and tighten the pinch bolt. If you find later that the headlamp bracket is a little loose, tighten this top nut a little more to pull the top yoke down.

15.24 Some models have chrome or painted bottom yoke or fork leg covers. Fit these now before inserting the fork legs.

THE REBUILD

The following procedure is for a Suzuki GT750A. Most makes and models use a similar method. Take note of this when dismantling your motorcycle.

15.25 Slip the fork legs into the bottom yoke to the approximate height of the top yoke.

15.26 Tighten them slightly to prevent them slipping out while you are fitting the headlamp brackets.

15.27 On this model, several parts are fitted with the headlamp bracket. This is the lower bracket rubber. It has to be fitted the correct way up. If it doesn't sit in the chrome cover snugly, then it is upside down, and must be turned over before the bracket is fitted.

15.28 Next, is the headlamp bracket lower supporting ring. This should fit nicely on the rubber.

15.29 Slide on the headlamp bracket.

15.30 Slide on the headlamp bracket top ring, making sure the rubber fits firmly like before.

15.31 Replace the top yoke and tap down firmly with a wooden or rubber mallet.

CLASSIC MOTORCYCLE RESTORATION

15.32 Slide the forks fully up to the top of the top yoke. Ensure they are flush with the top yoke, and fit the plastic covers.

15.34 Remember to fit any clock mounting rubbers.

15.35 Now fit any other rubbers that you have for the frame. Here, the fuel tank rubbers are being fitted to the frame.

15.33 Now tighten the bolts, being sure not to over-tighten them. The thread is usually in the top yoke, and we don't want to damage the thread here.

15.36 Two bolts hold the complete clock assembly in position.

THE REBUILD

15.37 The clocks are rubber-mounted, and need a good size washer on each side to prevent the nut pulling through.

15.39 Don't forget to fit the cable guides at this stage. Not all cables have them, but there are usually one or two for the speedometer or brake hose/cable.

15.40 If you have hydraulic brakes, the hose joint is almost certainly underneath the bottom yoke. This could also house your front brake switch. Bolt this on before the headlamp is fitted.

15.38 On this model the indicators are fitted to the headlamp brackets. On some models the indicators bolt directly to the headlamp bowl.

15.41 The headlamp rubbers should be fitted before the headlamp bowl. The rubbers are important, and prevent the cables wearing through on the edge of the metal headlamp bowl.

117

CLASSIC MOTORCYCLE RESTORATION

15.42 It is easier to push some of the loom connectors through the back of the headlamp just before bolting it in. The easiest way is to begin with the bigger connectors and work down in size until the last ones are single earth wires. If you push the connectors through randomly, it becomes difficult to push the larger connectors through the bunch of wires.

15.43 Make use of the cable holders, if you have them. It makes fitting the headlamp unit much easier.

15.44 Using two spanners, bolt the headlamp bowl onto the brackets.

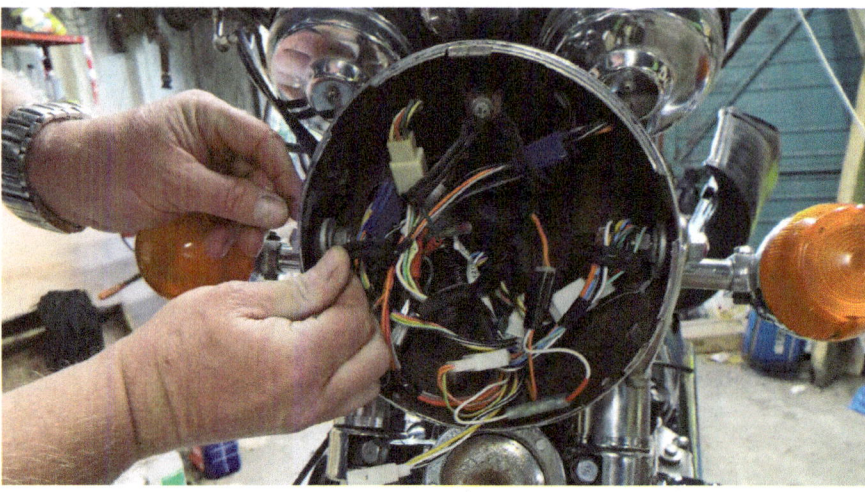

15.45 Pull all the wires through into the headlamp bowl, and secure to the side with the cable holders.

15.46 Plug in all of the block connectors and attach the wires to the headlamp unit.

15.47 Headlamps are usually clipped on at the top and pushed back neatly.

THE REBUILD

15.48 There are two, sometimes three, hidden screws that locate in the headlamp rim once it is pushed back. You may need to twist the lamp to line up the screw holes correctly.

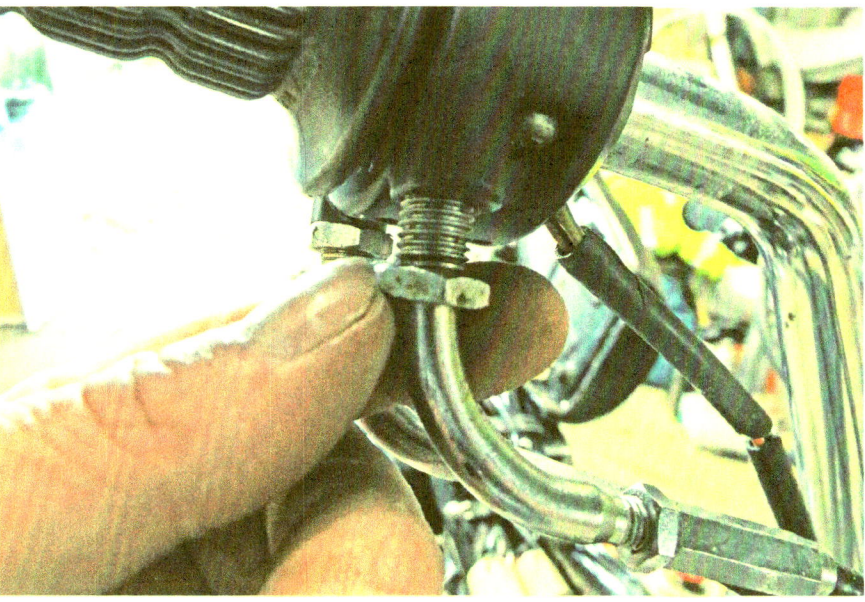

15.51 Screw in the throttle cable adjusters, but leave loose for now. These will need to be adjusted correctly when the other end of the cable is fitted to the carburettors.

15.49 Now fit the handlebars. Ensure that you line up the knurled part of the bars with the clamps. Set to the required position, then tighten the four bolts.

Once the handlebars are on, we can begin putting on the switchgear.

15.52 Thread through the cable nipples, and slide them into the holes on the twist grip.

15.50 Slide on the throttle twist grip. Note the two holes here for the throttle cable nipples. Some models will only have one hole.

15.53 Finally, firmly screw down the top of the switchgear with the two screws located underneath.

119

CLASSIC MOTORCYCLE RESTORATION

FITTING THE FRONT WHEEL

15.54 Now fit the front brake lever. If you have hydraulic brakes, bolt the master cylinder on now, too. Set the lever at an angle you feel comfortable with.

15.58 Before refitting the front wheel and front mudguard, ensure the speedometer drive is correctly located on the front wheel. Two metal tabs fit into the two slots.

15.61 Once the cable is in the correct position, tighten all the caps, making sure to use spring washers.

15.55 Tidy up the cabling. If you don't have the original cable ties, use tie wraps. Original cable ties are usually available.

15.59 Slide the front wheel spindle through the centre of the wheel, remembering to put the wheel spacers in the correct position.

15.62 Tighten the front mudguard stays, if the motorcycle has them. Fit the castle nut, remembering to fit a new split pin, too.

15.56 Fit the switchgear on the other side in the same way, along with the clutch lever. Place the cable nipple in the slot on the underside of the clutch lever.

15.60 Some forks have detachable bottom caps: keep these loose until the spindle is in the correct position.

15.63 If your motorcycle doesn't have the longer-type mudguard stays, the mudguard will be bolted to the fork legs, as seen here.

15.57 Line up the adjuster slots and push the cable into the slot. Once the cable is in, turn either of the adjusters so the cable doesn't fall out. We will adjust the clutch properly later.

15.64 Slide the front brake callipers over the brake disc, and bolt to the fork leg.

THE REBUILD

15.65 A trial fit of the seat and tank can give a good morale boost. We now can see the beginnings of a motorcycle again.

FITTING THE REAR WHEEL

Before refitting the rear wheel to the frame, the main components need to be put back together correctly. These components consist of the wheel, the sprocket carrier, and the brake hub. The rear brakes on most classic motorcycles are drum brakes. You may have a later model fitted with a rear disc brake. If you do, the disc bolts directly to the wheel. Installing the rear wheel and brake calliper on this type is the same as it was with the front wheel and brake calliper.

15.67 Check all bolts are tight and that there is no debris inside.

15.66 Check the rubber cush drive or shock absorber for wear. If it is damaged, replace it. Thankfully, most are in re-useable condition.

15.68 The sprocket carrier is then fitted, its lugs engaging with the cush drive slots. Here, a sprocket drum retainer can be seen, too.

15.69 The inside of this brake drum has a light layer of rust to clean off.

15.70 Using some 240 wet and dry paper, sand this back to a clean metal surface.

15.71 After a few minutes the brake drum is ready for the brake hub.

15.72 The new brake shoes, ready to be fitted.

CLASSIC MOTORCYCLE RESTORATION

15.73 These brake shoes are showing signs of scoring, and are lightly glazed.

15.76 Insert the rear wheel spindle to hold all parts in position.

15.79 Lift the rear wheel and push the spindle onto the swinging arm.

15.74 Although I would always recommend fitting new brake shoes, if these are not freely available a light rub down with some wet and dry paper removes the scoring and glaze, giving a useable brake shoe.
VERY IMPORTANT! Wear a dust mask here – some brake material contains asbestos, which is very dangerous if inhaled. This procedure should only be carried out if the brake shoe is not worn below the recommended wear limit.

15.77 Some models do not have an open-ended swinging arm. In this case, fit the rear wheel by lining up the spindle and sliding it through, remembering the wheel spacers.

15.80 This type of chain tensioner needs to be put on the spindle, before lifting it onto the swinging arm.

15.75 Place the brake hub inside the drum.

15.78 With the sprocket carrier fitted, it should look like this. Note here the rear wheel spindle has a small spacer in place, too.

15.81 Some models have a chain adjuster support, which needs to go in now.

THE REBUILD

15.82 Place the small cable locator in the drum brake cam lever.

15.83 On some models a split pin goes in here, too.

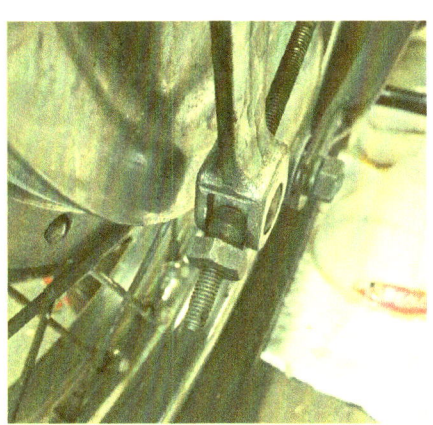

15.84 Screw on the rear brake cable/rod adjuster nut.

15.85 Fit the rear wheel torque arm to the brake hub. Always use a split pin here.

15.86 Adjust to the manufacturer's recommended setting. A split pin goes here after adjustment is complete.

15.87 The other end of the torque arm fits inside the bracket, and also has a split pin.

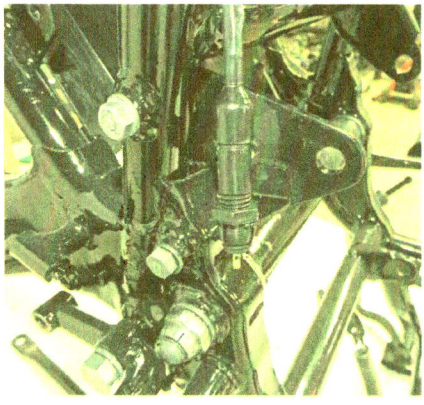

15.88 Here the engine mounting bracket has been fitted. On some motorcycles you may need to leave off one bracket from the frame to give more room when fitting the engine. If so, fit the mounting bracket after locating the engine correctly.

REFITTING THE ENGINE

With both wheels on, and the bike on the centre stand, we can put the engine back in. I would recommend you ask a friend to help with this. Even if you have a smaller engine, it can still cause injury if you drop it.

15.89 Most people can manage single-handed with a light engine like this. Even so, as a precaution it is best to have someone around when putting the engine back in the frame.

CLASSIC MOTORCYCLE RESTORATION

15.90 Refitting this size of engine is most certainly a two-person job.

15.95 Connect the HT caps to the sparkplugs.

15.91 Use a car jack to take the strain. Lift the engine onto a strong piece of wood to wheel into position.

15.93 With the engine in place, connect the earth strap. Ensure any paint is removed from the frame or engine where the earth strap connects.

15.96 Refit the carburettors.

15.92 Lift the engine off the wood onto another piece held in the frame. Reposition the jack so it is under the engine again, and slowly lower the engine until the engine mounting holes line up correctly. Put all the engine mounting bolts in position and tighten well. Remember any engine mounting rubbers.

15.94 Bolt on the HT coils.

15.97 Try to face all the jubilee clips in the same direction on each side, and line them up to give a uniform appearance.

THE REBUILD

15.98 If you have a 2-stroke motorcycle with an auto-lubrication system, connect the oil pump rod to the carburettors now. **IMPORTANT!** This must be set correctly, as described in the workshop manual, to give the required amount of oil when the engine is running.

15.101 Soft again, and much easier to put back on.

15.99 Put together all the parts of the air filter and fit a new filter element.

15.102 Now replace the air filter housing. On many motorcycles this sits inside the frame under the seat.

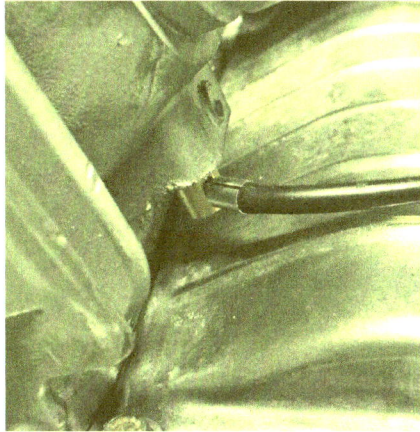

15.104 Remember to connect any oil lines to and from the oil pump.

15.100 If the air filter or carburettor filter rubbers have gone hard, soaking them in cellulose thinners for an hour will soften them.

15.103 Again, if you have a 2-stroke motorcycle with an auto-lubrication system, you can fit the oil tank now.

15.105 If the front sprocket was not fitted while the engine was on the bench, now is the time to do so. Remember to bend the locking washer against the nut.

CLASSIC MOTORCYCLE RESTORATION

15.106 Screw in the tachometer cable.

15.109 Connect the rear brake cable. This is a brake rod on some motorcycles.

15.112 A typical old drive chain. No amount of soaking in oil is going to restore this to useable condition.

15.107 If your bike has a radiator, put it back on.

15.110 Connect the spring to the brake lever and light switch, and adjust properly when the electrics are connected. The rear light should come on just as the brakes begin to hold the rear wheel.

15.113 In most cases the chain and sprockets are worn and in poor condition. I recommend fitting a new set. Try to get the correct sprocket sizes, to ensure gearing is as designed by the manufacturer.

15.108 Fit the rear brake lever..

15.111 If you have a brake cable, this fits into a slot cut on a frame bracket.

15.114 Place the chain on the rear sprocket, and feed it forward toward the front sprocket.

THE REBUILD

15.115 Ensure the engine is in neutral, and pull the chain over the top of the sprocket and all the way back, until the two ends meet in the middle.

15.118 Slide the split link onto the two slots as shown.

15.121 Now evenly adjust the two rear axle bolts until the wheel is straight and the chain has the recommended amount of movement.

15.116 Take the link and push through the two eyes in the end of the chain, completing the loop.

15.119 Making sure that the round end faces the direction of travel, tightly squeeze the end of the split link and one of the pins, until the open end of the split link is forced over the second slot.

15.122 On this model, 15-20mm (½-¾inch) of movement is recommended.

15.117 Place the other side of the link on the two link pins and push it back firmly, making sure the rear part of the link is pushed all the way through. You should see the slots in the pins at the ends.

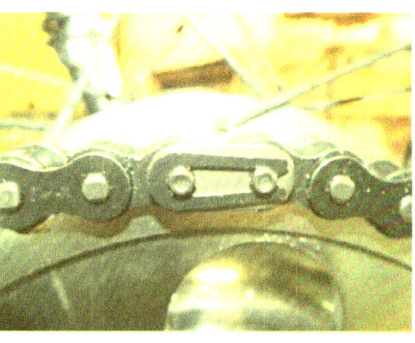

15.120 Once the link has been fitted, it should look like this. The split end has clipped firmly around the second pin.

15.123 When you are happy that the chain is set properly, fit the chain guard. There are usually two screws: one at either end.

CLASSIC MOTORCYCLE RESTORATION

FITTING THE EXHAUST

15.124 When fitting the exhaust system, always use new exhaust manifold gaskets. Use a little grease here on the gasket, to prevent it dropping out when you are positioning the front of the exhaust.

15.125 Fitting the exhaust is a two-handed job. Once the front of the exhaust is in position, try to insert a bolt in the rear bracket. This takes the strain while you finish bolting the exhaust to the engine.

15.126 Do not over-tighten the bolts. This is a common area for stripped threads. If later you find that the exhaust is blowing and you feel you've tightened enough, use another exhaust manifold gasket to prevent the blowing. It is common for these bolts to come loose after a while, so keep an eye on them.

15.127 Now put the seat back on, and slide in the two seat pins.

15.128 Insert the split pins, and open them so they cannot fall out.

15.129 With the seat back on, ensure it opens and closes properly, and that the seat catch and lock line up.

THE REBUILD

15.130 Your motorcycle should now look something like this; very close to being finished.

15.134 The side panels hook on at two points on the frame under the seat.

15.135 The side panels are then secured with a single screw at the bottom.

15.131 Put on the front sprocket cover.

15.133 Replace the side panels and tank, and screw on the badges.

15.136 Connect the fuel hose (and remember the hose clips to prevent the fuel leaking). Although not essential, it's a good idea to fit an inline fuel filter here (arrowed).

15.132 Refit the gearlever. Before tightening it, sit on the bike and ensure the lever is set at the correct angle. Also, ensure it is not too low, thus catching on the exhaust underneath.

CLASSIC MOTORCYCLE RESTORATION

With the main components all fitted, there are a few smaller items to be added to finish the rebuild. These vary from model to model, and should not be missed. Here are a few of the most common parts.

15.137 Most motorcycles have mirrors – well, at least one. They add to the overall original look, as well as give much better visibility.

15.140 Radiator cover. If the motorcycle is water-cooled, it almost certainly has a radiator cover to help protect the radiator from damage.

15.138 Brake hose brackets. If the bike has disc brakes, there will be some sort of bracket to hold the hose firmly.

15.141 Fuel cap cover. Often this is simply a fuel cap with a lock, but some motorcycles have a separate flap, as can be seen in this photo.

15.139 Speedo cable guide: there to prevent the cable from catching on the front wheel.

15.142 With the additional parts now fitted, the rebuild is complete.

Chapter 16
Getting ready for the road

Getting this far in the restoration grants you a well-deserved pat on the back. By now you should have what looks like a very respectable motorcycle. It may not be perfect yet – as I've said, some spare parts are often difficult to source, and you may have had to continue with a part that you would have really rather changed – but you are almost there, and ready to set up the bike.

All of the main components are now in place, and the motorcycle almost ready to ride. There are a few settings and adjustments that need to be carried out at this stage. The detailed settings are in the workshop manual, but many are common to most motorcycles, and these are what I go through in this chapter. First though, check over all the nuts, bolts, and screws to ensure they are tight. It is very easy to have missed one, so check now.

CABLES

The first point to mention about cables, be they clutch or brake, is to ensure that you have the correct ones for your motorcycle. Pattern parts are fine, but cables from another make or model won't do. The cable length, type of nipples, and adjusters can differ from one motorcycle to another.

All of the cables on your motorcycle have adjusters. Some have one at each end. These are to help you set the correct amount of tension or slack on the cable.

16.1 Looking first at the clutch cable – a good starting point is to aim for around 3-4mm (⅛th inch) of slack at the clutch lever. This ensures that the clutch is fully engaged and will not slip when riding. If the clutch cable is too tight, it slightly disengages the clutch, leading to the clutch slipping and early wear. Use the cable adjuster at the clutch lever end of the cable to set the slack, but never unscrew it so much that it is on the limit of the thread.

16.2 If you need to unscrew the cable this much, equalise the amount of adjustment at the other end of the cable. If this is not possible, it is likely that the cable is the incorrect length. Only on riding the motorcycle will you know whether the clutch is adjusted properly, but if the clutch plates are in good condition, with 3-4mm (⅛ inch) of slack at the clutch lever, I would say that your clutch is now adjusted correctly and should work fine.

CLASSIC MOTORCYCLE RESTORATION

16.5 Both ends of the cables should be locked with the locking nuts when the desired setting is reached.

16.3 Now onto the brake cables – this is usually set up similar to the clutch cable, with 25mm (1 inch) of slack at the lever. That is to say, you should be able to pull back the lever by approximately that amount (for front brakes). There should be some movement possible on the brake lever before the brakes begin to hold the wheel. This area of movement is where the brake light should be set to come on, just a fraction before the brake is engaged. The rear brake is adjusted in a similar fashion. Hydraulic disc front brakes usually need no adjustment at the lever, although some models do have an adjuster bolt to set lever travel. Adjustment is also carried out at the brake calliper, to take up any wear in the front disc pads – not to adjust the position of the brake lever.

BRAKE LIGHTS

The throttle cable should be free-moving, and should snap back under spring pressure when released after opening to the full throttle position. The cable should have 1mm of free play at the carburettor end. If it has been routed correctly, this amount should not alter when the handlebars are turned to full lock in both directions.

16.6 The adjuster is used to set the correct cable length, not to adjust the engine speed.

MIRRORS

Setting the mirrors correctly is a simple but important procedure to carry out. Some motorcycles only have one mirror, but most have one on each side of the handlebars.

16.4 It is often the case that the rear brake light spring needs to be shortened, so that the brakelight can be adjusted properly. If you come across this, simply snip off the required amount and bend the end again to the original shape.

16.7 Sitting on the motorcycle while it is off the stands, set the mirrors so that you cannot see your own reflection – you may not completely achieve this, but you need to see as much of the road and traffic behind you as possible. Try to set the mirrors to view slightly different distances.

16.8 Once they are set, tighten the locknuts – you don't want them to move while you are riding.

GETTING READY FOR THE ROAD

TYRE PRESSURE AND TREAD
Check that the tyre pressures match that set by the manufacture, and that the tyres are not worn.

SPLIT PINS
Recheck that all castle nuts have split pins in, and that the split pin has been bent open.

LIGHTS
Check that all of the lights are working, and that the headlight beam is set to the correct angle. Each country has different height requirements – check your local regulations, and adjust accordingly, following these steps:

The bike needs to be facing a wall so that, when the light is turned on, you can see where the beam is and can measure it. The motorcycle should be 3.81m away from the wall. Ask someone to sit on the bike and hold it up straight. Measure the height of the bulb from ground level – in the UK, the setting of the beam is different depending on whether the bulb is higher or lower than 850mm.

Draw a horizontal line on the wall at the same height as your headlight bulb. This line will be called the 'horizontal zero per cent line.' Next, draw a line up from the ground, crossing the centre of the horizontal zero per cent line, and extending about 300mm past it. This line is the 'vertical zero per cent line.'

Ensure that the tyres are correctly inflated, as this affects the height of the bike.

Bulbs below 850mm from the ground
If the centre of the motorbike's headlight bulb is less than 850mm from the ground, the top of the dipped beam should be between 20mm to 80mm below the horizontal zero per cent line.

Bulbs above 850mm from the ground
In this instance, the top of the dipped beam should be between 50mm and 110mm below the horizontal zero per cent line.

If your beam isn't within the tolerances, adjust it until it does fall within tolerance by loosening the two headlamp bolts for up/down movement. If your bike is within the tolerances, the next step is to check the beam's positioning against the vertical zero per cent line.

16.9 Most motorcycles have a screw in the headlight chrome ring allowing for easy sideways adjustment.

Most UK bikes have a headlight that lifts up to the left. It is important that this lift-up doesn't begin immediately from the vertical zero per cent line. Ensure there is a gap of around 100mm between the vertical zero per cent line and the area where your headlight begins to kick up.

FIRST START-UP
As tempting as it is to just start the motorbike, first you must make some essential checks.

Check the oil is to the correct level. Put in fresh fuel, and, if the bike is a 2-stroke model, check the 2-stroke oil, too.

Did you fit new sparkplugs? If not, are they clean, correctly gapped and showing a spark? Is the battery fully charged. If the engine is water-cooled, is the coolant filled to the correct level?

16.10 Turn on the ignition.

16.11 Set the choke to the 'on' position.

16.12 Ensure the engine kill switch is in the 'run' position, and turn the fuel tap to the 'on' position.

Ensure it is not in gear, and give it a kick on the kickstart, or press the starter. Slightly open the throttle each time you try. It may take a few attempts, especially if the engine has been rebuilt, but after two or three tries it should fire. Once it fires and begins to run, just let it warm a little before opening the throttle any more. If you open the throttle too early the engine will flood, making it more difficult to start next time.

After it has run on tick over for a minute or two, slowly open the throttle

CLASSIC MOTORCYCLE RESTORATION

to bring the revs up. This warms the engine quicker, and gets it up to running temperature.

Does it sound okay? Watch out for any leaks, especially petrol. If there is a leak, it needs to be stopped quickly. The most common at this stage is the carburettors overflowing, because the valve in the float bowl has not been seated properly or a tiny piece of dirt is preventing it from closing. Try a gentle tap with a piece of wood on the float bowl – this often solves the problem. If you have no leaks, that's great.

Does the engine settle to a nice tick over if you open then close the throttle? It often takes several attempts at setting the carburettors before the engine runs evenly at the correct RPM.

If the engine does not misfire, ticks over okay, and revs cleanly, it sounds like you've done a good job setting it up. Well done.

THE FIRST RIDE

If the bike is running well, take it out for its maiden ride. Ensure you have all the legal requirements in place beforehand.

Go through all the basic maintenance checks recommended by the manufacturer, including:
- Check the engine/gearbox oil level
- Check the 2-stroke oil level
- Check the brake fluid level
- Check the front and rear brakes are correctly adjusted
- Check the chain tension
- Lubricate the chain
- Check that all the lights and indicators work correctly
- Ensure you have enough fuel to complete your ride
- Check the clutch lever play

If the bike is water-cooled:
- Check the coolant level
- Check for leaks

On your first run, don't go too far – there are usually teething troubles after any rebuild, and you don't want to break down miles away from home. A couple of laps around the block is enough, then come back and check that everything is okay. Slowly increase the range of the rides as you gain confidence that the newly rebuilt bike is not going to break down.

If the engine has been rebuilt, remember to run it in as recommended by the manufacturer. Everything is new and tight, and needs some gentle miles on the clock before you use the full rev range.

Remember, usually after a short running-in period the cylinder head bolts and exhaust bolts need to be torqued again (check with your workshop manual). Once this has been done, just keep an eye on fluid levels and you are finished!

Chapter 17
Riding safely

It is a chilling fact that motorcycles comprise less than 1% of vehicle traffic, but their riders suffer 14% of total deaths and serious injuries on Britain's roads (DETR, 2000). This pattern is repeated in many countries across the world. Following some basic guidance and attending a rider training course greatly helps you stay safe on the roads.

Many first time restorers are restoring motorcycles that they had in their youth. The lucky amongst you will still be in your youth. For one reason or another, you may have given up motorcycling years ago, and, like me, never really lost your love for it. We got better jobs, met girlfriends, got married and had families, then spent a good deal of time out of the saddle. Things have changed a lot since then, and we all need to take more care out on the roads. Whether you are a seasoned rider, new to motorcycling, or returning to it, make your safety a priority.

When I first had motorcycles there were far fewer cars on the road than there are now. I remember playing football in the road as a teenager. My friends and I had to get out of the way of the odd car that was passing. You could never play football in that same road now. Even in a small village setting, it is very busy with a constant stream of traffic.

My advice to anyone who hasn't ridden a motorcycle for a while is to go out on your first few rides at quiet times of the day or weekends. Try going out earlier or later in the day on Sundays, when the traffic hasn't really started yet, or after the Sunday afternoon rush has died down. These are the best times for your first few rides. Go out on a nice sunny day, and keep a check on the weather forecast.

A COUNTRY ROAD STORY
I remember the first time I rode a bike having not been in the saddle for a while. It was an eye opener. I thought I knew how to ride – I knew I *used* to know how to ride – but it soon became clear I had to almost learn again.

After a short journey, I noticed I was taking a wider line than necessary on corners. I found that bends just seem to get tighter and tighter, and that I was going much further out than I was comfortable with – almost to the opposite side of the road. That country road trip suddenly didn't seem so appealing, with the tractor heading in my direction and me almost in his lane. I pulled back in time, but it certainly gave me a wake-up call.

I remembered the long rides with my pals, but I had forgotten that there were slippery manhole covers, white lines, cat's eyes, and potholes to negotiate. I realised on this first short journey that I really did need to take things easy and get used to riding again, then I would be able to enjoy my motorcycling, the way I remembered it.

Think about joining a club if you can. All clubs welcome new members and have regular club ride-outs. It is easy for a car driver not to see a lone motorcyclist, but not so easy to miss a group of them. Remember the old saying: safety in numbers.

17.1 Clubs often carry out important voluntary work. These guys deliver emergency blood supplies for local hospitals.

CLASSIC MOTORCYCLE RESTORATION

17.2 This group has medically trained volunteers in rural areas who can attend the scene of an accident and offer initial treatment before the ambulance arrives.

Wear appropriate clothing and buy the best you can afford. Ensure you have a good pair of motorcycle boots, a good jacket, trousers, gloves, and a crash helmet.

Be seen – wear a high visibility vest or jacket, and keep the headlamp on at all times, day or night.

Keep a simple all-weather kit under your seat. Even in the summer you can get caught out, and once you are wet, the rest of the ride will be miserable.

Learn to ride defensively. Expect every car, van, truck or even another motorcycle to pull out in front of you at junctions. Be ready with your brakes, and drive carefully past junctions.

Keep a safe distance between you and the vehicle in front, and alternatively, if the vehicle behind is a little too close, make some space for yourself.

If you are filtering between rows of traffic, watch out for other vehicles changing lanes. This is most likely to happen when a junction change is coming up. The driver realises they are in the incorrect lane, they don't look properly, and change direction quickly. You don't want to be there when that happens. I was riding an old Honda Goldwing one time, between the traffic at slow speed. A driver noticed that his car door wasn't closed properly, and, just as I approached, he opened the door quickly and slammed it shut. I almost crashed into the open car door – another close shave.

OVERTAKING

Some of these are obvious, but I will mention them anyway.

Do not overtake at junctions, pedestrian crossings, hills or bends. The classic accident is the rider who is overtaking a car that has failed to indicate, and turns just as the motorcycle pulls alongside. Beware. There will be only one winner here.

BAD ROAD CONDITIONS

It is said that motorcyclists who have off-road riding experience, such as motorcross or trials riding, are safer riders than those who have not. The reason is that in these sports the riding surface is changing all the time, from muddy soil, to wet slopes, to sand or slippery rocks. The rider learns to change their riding style to suit the conditions, and he or she needs to react quickly. This is a useful skill, and should be used by all riders. Look out for tell-tale signs of potential hazards.

Keep a check on the road surface conditions. A diesel spill is very common on corners and roundabouts, and very dangerous for a motorcyclist. It looks like a shiny wet line on dry roads, or like shimmering colours of the rainbow on wet roads. Look out ahead for muddy roads and leaves, and be aware that, on rural roads, grain spills are like marbles to a motorcyclist.

If there is a shower after a long dry spell, the road surface will be more slippery than normal. This is because it has a thin covering of rubber, worn from the tyres of other traffic. The new rain shower sits on the rubber and makes for a very slippery surface.

17.3 This thin line of spilt diesel spells danger for a motorcyclist.

RIDING SAFELY

Once the rain has washed this away the road will improve a little, but it will still be slippery simply because it is wet.

Lastly on road conditions, keep a good check on your tyres. Ensure they have good tread and are inflated to the correct pressure.

TRAINING
Almost all countries have safety organisations that offer training and advice for motorcyclists. These are well worth looking into and getting involved with. The UK has the Bike Safe Scheme, and in the USA there are courses run by the Motorcycling Safety Foundation. Most countries have similar safety schemes set up for motorcyclists.

Enjoy your riding, and be safe!

17.4 A rain shower after a dry spell, and tell-tale signs of a slippery road surface.

17.6 Safety is in everyone's interests, and is promoted at most motorcycle events.

ALSO FROM VELOCE –

ISBN: 978-1-845847-46-3
Paperback • 27x20.7cm • 176 pages • 682 colour pictures

Gives enthusiasts of the single overhead cam Honda 4 a step-by-step guide to a full restoration, whether it be the small but luxurious CB350/4 or the ground breaking CB750/4. This guide covers dismantling the motorcycle and its components, restoring and sourcing parts, paint spraying, decals and polishing.

For more info on Veloce titles, visit our website at www.veloce.co.uk • email: info@veloce.co.uk
• Tel: +44(0)1305 260068

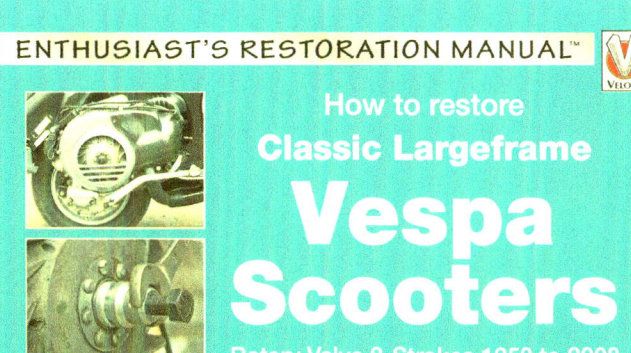

ISBN: 978-1-787110-28-1
Paperback • 27x20.7cm • 160 pages
• 878 colour and b&w pictures

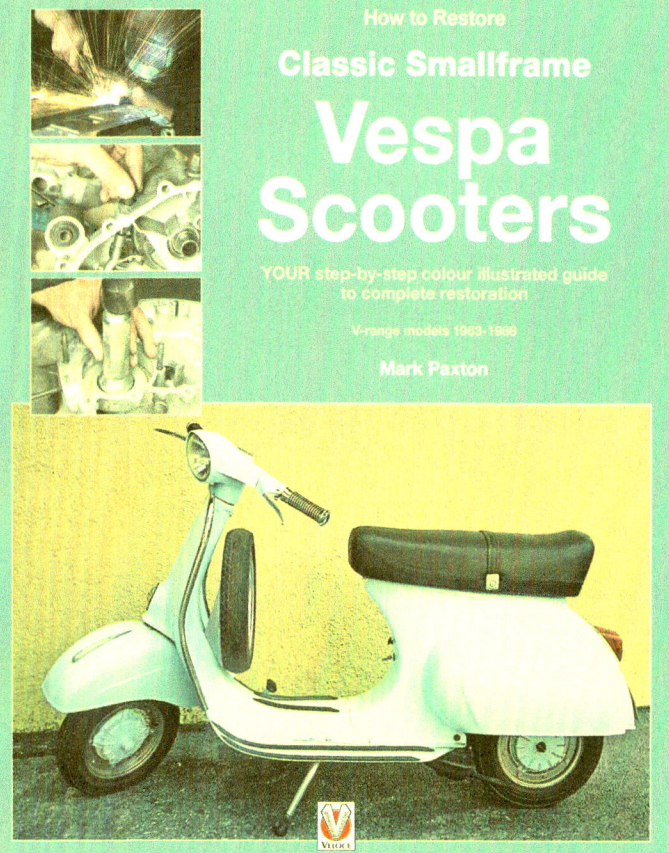

These books investigate the reality of Vespa restoration in detail. Aimed at the do-it-yourself enthusiast and each featuring hundreds of clear colour photographs, these are essential step-by-step guides to the complete renovation of your beloved scooter.

ISBN: 978-1-787114-08-1
Paperback • 27x20.7cm • 120 pages
• 688 colour and b&w pictures

ALSO FROM VELOCE –

ISBN: 9-781-845841-34-8

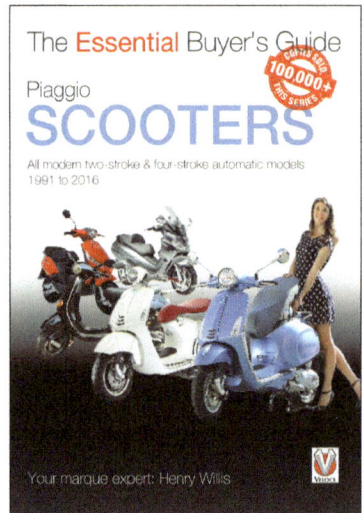
ISBN: 9-78-1-845849-92-4

ISBN: 9-781-845842-84-0

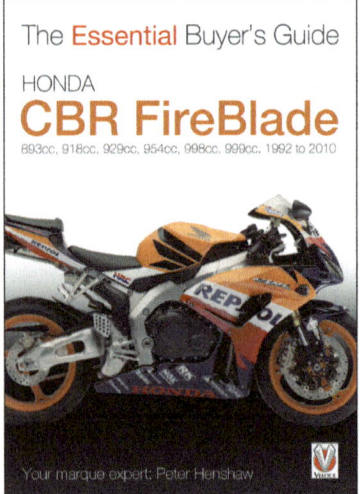
ISBN: 9-781-845843-07-6

ISBN: 9-78-1-787116-52-8

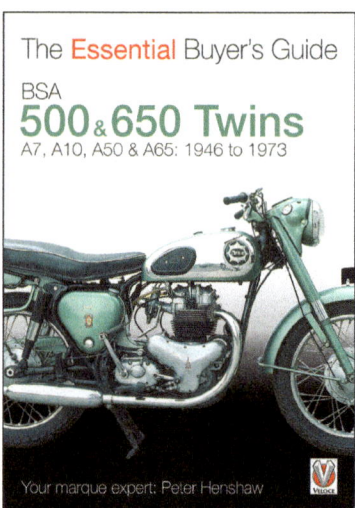
ISBN: 9-781-845841-36-2

ISBN: 9-781-845843-03-8

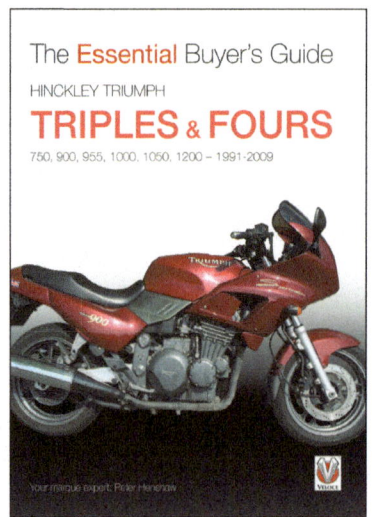
ISBN: 9-781-845842-87-1

ISBN: 9-781-845841-35-5

ISBN: 9-781-845843-0-0

ISBN: 9-781-845843-63-2

ISBN: 978-1-787114-72-2

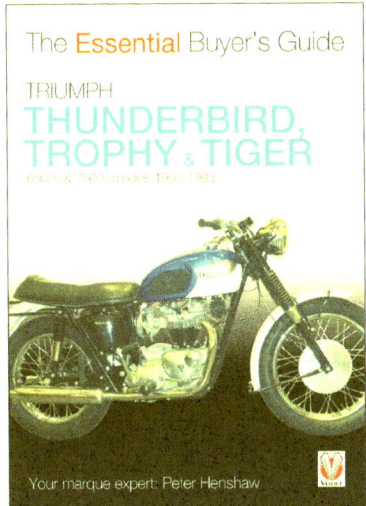
ISBN: 9-781-845846-09-1

ISBN: 9-78-1-845848-83-5

ISBN: 9-781-845845-23-0

ISBN: 9-781-845846-55-8

ISBN: 9-781-845845-67-4

Having one of these books in your pocket is just like having a real marque expert at your side. Benefit from the author's years of ownership experience, learn how to spot a bad bike quickly, and how to assess a promising bike like a professional. Get the right bike at the right price!

Paperback • 19.5x13.9cm • 64 pages • c100 colour pictures

ALSO FROM VELOCE –

ISBN: 978-1-787111-81-3
Paperback • 27x20.7cm • 288 pages
• 1290 colour and b&w pictures

Ducati's classic 750, 860, 900 and Mille bevel-drive twins from 1971-1986 are now amongst the most collectable bikes in the world. This book serves as a definitive guide to authenticity, and gives hands-on restoration tips and guidance.

For more info on Veloce titles, visit our website at www.veloce.co.uk • email: info@veloce.co.uk
• Tel: +44(0)1305 260068

Index

Air filter 70
Alternator 82
Auto jumble 27, 28

Badges 87, 89, 90
Baffles 74, 75
Battery 29, 78
Bearings, head stock 113
Brake adjustment 123, 126, 132
Brake caliper 57, 58, 59, 120
Brake disk 59, 63
Brake hose 57, 130
Brake master cylinder 59, 61, 62
Brake piston 58, 59
Brake shoes 121, 122

Cabinet blaster 44
Cables 119, 132
Camshaft 54
Carburettor 32, 70, 71, 72 , 73, 124
Carburettor rubbers 70
Chain 126, 127
Clutch 49, 50
Clutch adjustment 131
Clutch plates 23
Coil 81, 124
Clocks 35, 94, 95, 96, 97
Clubs 26
Compression 51
Crankshaft 55, 56
Cush drive 121
Cylinder 23, 52, 53
Cylinder head 29, 52, 53, 76

Decals 87, 89, 90
Decarbonisation 53
Duck 66

Engine 52, 124
Exhaust 74, 76128

Filler 86
Filter, air 32, 125
Filter, oil 48
Fire extinguisher 9
First aid 8
Flasher unit 82
Foot rests 113
Fork oil 109
Fork seal 107, 108, 109
Forks 24, 25, 36 , 105, 106, 107
Frame 24, 36, 37, 39, 110
Fuel filter 129
Fuel tank 24, 31, 67, 68, 88, 89, 130
Fuel tap 29, 68, 69, 70
Fuse 80

Gaskets 48
Gear shaft 48, 129

Headlamp 118, 119, 133
Honda 6, 8, 19-21, 27, 35, 46, 47, 70, 73, 76, 88, 90, 98, 104, 136
HT cap 81

Ignition, contact breaker points 80, 81
Importing 21

Indicators 33
Inner tube 64
Internet 26

Jets, carburettor 72

Kickstart 48

Light, rear 112
Lock, seat 112

Mirrors 130, 132
Mudguard 33, 34, 112, 120

Oil 49
Oil, 2-stroke 125
Oil tank 51 125
Overtaking 136

Paint 85
Paint stripping 85
Piston and rings 23, 52, 53, 54
Polishing 41-43
Preparation 37
Primer 85

Road conditions 136, 137
Rubbers 31, 116, 117, 125

Safety wear 9
Seals 55
Seat 24, 25, 31, 98, 99, 100, 101, 103, 104, 128

CLASSIC MOTORCYCLE RESTORATION

Seat cover 98, 99, 101, 103
Seat trim 102, 103
Shock absorber 111
Side panels 32, 129
Solenoid 82
Sparkplug 29 , 81
Spraying 39, 86, 87, 92, 96
Stands 111
Starter motor 83

Stripe 88, 89, 90
Swinging arm 30, 36, 110,
Swinging arm bushes 110
Switchgear 35, 91, 92, 93, 94, 119

Tap and die 16, 103
Torque 51
Torque arm 123
Tyres 64, 65, 66

Ultrasonic cleaner 41, 69

Valves 54
Voltage regulator 82

Wheels 35, 63, 65, 66, 120, 122
Wiring 34, 78, 79, 80, 112, 118